Marxists Against Stalinism
A debate with Chris Harman

Ernest Mandel

Preface by Paul Le Blanc

Resistance Books
International Institute for Research and Education

Edited by Alex de Jong and Fred Leplat
Design and layout by Adam Di Chiara

Cover photo: Hofbauer Róbert (cc), head of Joseph Stalin's statue, Budapest during Hungarian Revolution, 1956.

ISBN 978-0-902869-64-6

Published 2022 by Resistance Books (London) and the International Institute for Research and Education (Amsterdam).

Marxists against Stalinism is issue 72 of the Notebooks for Study and Research published by the International Institute for Research and Education.

Our thanks go to the Ernest Mandel Internet Archive and the Ernest Mandel Study Centre at the International Institute for Research and Education (IIRE) in Amsterdam. Their on-going work to gather Mandel's work in its many languages is worthy of your support.

We invite readers to visit iire.org and donate to the effort.

Contents

Preface: Revolutionary Marxism and late Soviet realities

Ernest Mandel's confrontation with state capitalist theory

Paul Le Blanc

This volume presents a confrontation between two outstanding figures in late twentieth-century Marxist thought, Ernest Mandel (1923-1995) and Chris Harman (1942-2009).

Essential aspects of Mandel's contributions to Marxist thought are presented in our previous volume of his writings, *Introduction to Marxist Theory*. He is most widely known for his economic analyses: *Marxist Economic Theory, The Formation of the Economic Thought of Karl Marx, Late Capitalism, Long Waves of Capitalist Development*, as well as his very substantial introductions to the three volumes of Marx's *Capital* produced by the editors of the journal *New Left Review* in widely-distributed paperback editions in 1977-1981. A leading figure in the Fourth International, a federation of revolutionary socialist groups founded in the 1930s by Leon Trotsky and his co-thinkers, he wrote two influential studies on Trotsky's thought: *Trotsky, A Study in the Dynamic of His Thought* and *Trotsky as Alternative*.[1]

Chris Harman is perhaps best known for his massive survey *A People's History of the World*, but significant contributions to historical writing are also to be found in *The Lost Revolution: Germany 1918-1923* and *Class Struggles in Eastern Europe 1945-1983*. In addition to a significant body of historical and political analyses, he developed searching economic studies, the primary example being his last major work, *Zombie Capitalism: Global Crisis and the Relevance of Marx*. Like Mandel, Harman devoted most of his life to building the revolutionary socialist movement. He was part of the International Socialist political current (culminating in the British Socialist Workers Party), led by Tony Cliff. This originated in a split from the Fourth International in the early 1950s, around the particular variant of 'state capitalist' theory developed by Cliff.[2]

Rooted in the rich traditions of revolutionary Marxism, both Mandel and Harman were unrelentingly anti-Stalinist – insistent on the inseparability of actual socialism from genuine workers' democracy – influenced by the perspectives of Leon Trotsky. Like Trotsky, but unlike certain elements on the left, their anti-Stalinism did not cause them to align with the essentially imperialist foreign policy of 'the West' in the global Cold War power struggle. Nor did they align with what some called 'the socialist camp' (headed by the Soviet Union), whose pretentions of actual socialism both men saw as a travesty. Each favoured a revolution that could bring genuine socialism to the Soviet Union and similar countries – but embedded in this last position was the fundamental difference that divided Mandel and Harman from each other.

Mandel favoured what Trotsky had urged: a *political revolution*, which would break the stranglehold of the privileged bureaucratic elite over the nationalized and planned economy and establish democratic control by the majority of labouring people over the economy. For him, in what Trotsky had considered a 'degenerated workers' state' there remained important elements from 'the conquests of the October Revolution' – and these were worth defending even amid the struggle against the privileged bureaucracy. Harman, on the other hand, was convinced that Trotsky had failed to comprehend the crystallization in the Soviet Union of a variant of capitalism (what he saw as state-capitalism), requiring a more thoroughgoing *social revolution*. The notion that the Soviet Union could possibly represent any kind of 'workers' state' was anathema to the partisans of the state-capitalism analysis.[3]

This volume presents a set of polemics in which these comrades seek to comprehend and explain the nature of the realities facing those who seek to change the world. In this introductory essay, we will indicate the historical and theoretical context of the debate, explore key aspects of Trotsky's analysis of the nature and trajectory of post-revolutionary Soviet society, and conclude with a brief reflection on the Mandel-Harman debate.

Contexts of the state capitalism debate

Mandel's arguments are inseparable not only from Trotsky's perspectives of the 1930s, but also from his own empirical studies and analyses of later decades – for example, in two of his three last major works, *Beyond Perestroika* and *Money and Power* (the other being his searching reaffirmation *Trotsky as Alternative*). Such studies form a literary contextual frame within which his polemics on state-capitalism must be situated.[4]

Historical actualities – the world's first socialist revolution, and what became of it – were essential to the debate. Russia's October revolution of 1917, led by Lenin and Trotsky, establishing the power of the soviets (democratic workers' councils), was seen as providing a pathway to the liberation of humanity. The realities turned out to be more complex and problematical than had originally been hoped, however. The October Revolution led not to the liberation of humanity but to a new form of tyranny, and this compelled theorists and activists to explain what had happened and why, and what this might mean for practical work in the future.[5]

Mandel was hardly working out his thinking in isolation, active as he was in a global political collective, the Fourth International, collaborating with vibrant national sections and numerous thinkers and activists sharing experiences, analyses and perspectives.[6] Harman also had collaborators in the International Socialists, and eventually the Socialist Workers Party, advancing sharp criticisms against the Fourth International, whose partisans responded in kind.[7]

These polemics are part of a broader context explored by Marcel van der Linden in *Western Marxism and the Soviet Union*. Van der Linden surveys more than a hundred contending Marxist-influenced analyses which rejected the Stalinist view that some kind of 'socialism' existed in the Soviet Union. Most fell within three broad categories: (1) **degenerated workers' state**, seeing Soviet society as an unstable and bureaucratically deformed formation nonetheless having the potential of leading to socialism; (2) **state capitalist**, seeing Soviet society as a variant of capitalism which must simply be overturned and replaced with socialism; (3) **bureaucratic collectivist**, seeing a new form of class society, neither capitalist nor socialist, which should be replaced with democratic government and a socialist economy. While none of these approaches are fully consistent with what van der Linden refers to as 'orthodox Marxism', he adds that none of them have proved capable of adequately analysing the complex phenomenon of Soviet society – conceding, however, that each can generate useful insights.[8]

Van der Linden and others have documented that a number of different conceptualizations of 'state capitalism' have emerged over the years: among Mensheviks and dissident Bolsheviks in the early 1920s, among those associated with the council communist current (Gorter, Pannekoek, Rühle, Korsch, Mattick), among others associated with Austro-Marxism (Friedrich Adler, Otto Bauer), as well as Amadeo Bordiga, Charles Bettelheim, Paul Sweezy, Richard Wolff, and others. Coming out of the Trotskyist tradition, significant 'state capitalist' analyses have been articulated by Manuel Fernández-Grandizo (commonly known as G. Munis), C.L.R. James and Raya Dunayevskaya, Cornelius Castoriadis, Claude Lefort – as well as Tony Cliff and such co-thinkers as Chris Harman.[9]

One might suggest that the relatively open yet critical-minded approach expressed by van der Linden is consistent with the way Trotsky's own analysis developed. As Thomas Twiss documents in his remarkable study *Trotsky and the Problem of Soviet Bureaucracy*, Trotsky's classic *The Revolution Betrayed* was the culmination of an ongoing process of theoretical reformulation and innovation, progressing beyond tentative formulations and false starts, driven by his ongoing engagement with evolving and complex realities.[10]

I. Trotsky as reference point

Trotsky's *Revolution Betrayed* was completed in 1936. Like the *Communist Manifesto*, it is densely packed with ideas. As with the manifesto of Marx and Engels, successive readings of Trotsky's book yield new insights that often have a startling contemporary relevance. This central reference point for both Mandel and Harman merits closer examination here.[11]

Academic Robert H. McNeal once claimed in an influential essay that, despite 'a lot of writing about Stalinism over many years,' Trotsky simply 'could not come to terms with the cruel irony that confronted him in Stalin's Russia and Comintern,' because it contradicted his deep belief 'in human progress, most particularly in the progressive meaning of his life as a revolutionary.[12] After all, the vision of socialism (or communism) advanced by Marx and Engels posited a free association of producers in which there would flourish the free development of all. Lenin and Trotsky led the Bolsheviks to power in the Russian Revolution of 1917 precisely in the name of this liberating vision, yet the eventual product of the revolution was the system of Stalin.

Across the political spectrum – even among those willing to admit that the Bolshevik revolution involved a profoundly democratic upsurge of working people – this line of argument has been employed to demonstrate that Stalin is Lenin's 'true heir,' that the Bolshevik tradition of revolutionary Marxism logically leads to totalitarianism.

Responding to this challenge is of crucial importance particularly for those who are committed to a socialist revolution. If Bolshevik perspectives can actually lead to a socialism of freedom and community instead of to a bureaucratic dictatorship, then the phenomenon of Stalinism should be most adequately explained by a Bolshevik analysis, one that is true to the liberating conception of socialism contained in the *Communist Manifesto* and Lenin's *State and Revolution*.

From a Bolshevik standpoint, it is absolutely essential to develop such an analysis in order to guide one's practical political work. Contrary to Robert McNeal's assertion, this was a primary task which Trotsky set for himself in *The Revolution Betrayed*, developing a critique of Stalinism and the nature of Soviet society that could at one and the same time be faithful to the facts and to the revolutionary socialist goal. The commitment to the goal was a key to developing the most profound analysis – it is impossible to understand things as they are without having a sense of how they can and should be.

Trotsky's summary of *The Revolution Betrayed*

Trotsky's study begins, in the very first paragraph of the first chapter, by summarizing his theory of permanent revolution, and also the underlying law of uneven and combined development. This provides the broad foundation of his analysis. The democratic revolution against the tyrannical tsarist system in Russia could only be accomplished by the working class. This would put political power in the hands of the working class, which would propel the policies of the new regime in a socialist direction. The international factor would immediately come into play, not simply in the form of military hostility against the infant Soviet Republic by the world's capitalist governments, but in the form of innumerable and profound pressures of the world capitalist economy on the daily life of the Soviet peoples. Trotsky observes that the future of socialism, not to mention the very survival of the country and its population, required that it 'catch up' with the level of economic development of the advanced industrial countries. Throughout the book he also stresses another aspect of the international factor: the development of socialism in the USSR was dependent on the success of socialist revolutions in other countries, especially more advanced industrial countries.

'The extraordinary tardiness in the development of the international revolution, upon whose prompt aid the leaders of the Bolshevik party had counted, created immense difficulties for the Soviet Union, but also revealed its inner powers and resources,' Trotsky noted. Reviewing gains in industrial and cultural development, accomplished through the planned economy and the idealistic energy of a great many people, he added that, even if there were to be an eventual collapse of the USSR, 'there would remain as an earnest of the future this indestructible fact, that thanks solely to a proletarian revolution a backward country has achieved in less than ten years successes unexampled in history.'[13]

Yet socialism was predicated upon the ability of a technologically developed economy to provide a decent life for all, and also upon a significant degree of harmonious economic cooperation among nations. It could not exist in the economically backward USSR, despite glowing propaganda of the Stalin regime. 'Law can never be higher than the economic structure and the cultural development of society conditioned by that structure,' Trotsky quoted from Marx, following up with another Marx quote: 'A development of the productive forces is the absolutely necessary practical premise [of communism], because without it want is generalized, and with want the struggle for necessities begins again, and that means that all the old crap must revive.'[14]

Unlike many superficial analysts, Trotsky did not base his analysis of 'what went wrong' on the evil designs of Joseph Stalin. He identifies the problem as developing before Stalin's dictatorship was consolidated. He notes that in the midst of foreign intervention, civil war, and economic collapse, 'democracy had been narrowed in proportion as difficulties increased. In the beginning, the [Bolshevik, or Communist] party had wished and hoped to preserve freedom of political struggle within the framework of the Soviets [democratic councils]. The civil war introduced stern amendments into this calculation. The opposition parties were forbidden one after the other. This measure, obviously in conflict with the spirit of Soviet democracy, the leaders of Bolshevism regarded not as a principle, but as an episodic act of self-defence.'[15]

Instead, he notes, democracy soon disappeared in the party itself, as well as in the soviets, in the trade unions, the cooperatives, cultural organizations, etc. 'Above each and every one of them there reigns an unlimited hierarchy of party secretaries.'[16] This was not generated by some 'fatal flaw' in Bolshevism or Lenin's ideas, he insists, but by something more fundamental that developed during the civil war period and the early years of the New Economic Policy (from 1918 through the early 1920s). The dynamic is captured in this passage:

> The basis of bureaucratic rule is the poverty of society in objects of consumption, with the resulting struggle of each against all. When there are enough goods in a store, the purchasers can come whenever they want to. When there are few goods, the purchasers are compelled to stand in line. When the lines are very long, it is necessary to appoint a policeman to keep order. Such is the starting point of the power of the bureaucracy. It 'knows' who is to get something and who has to wait.[17]

Trotsky's summary provides a useful checklist of nine key points:

> The Soviet Union is a contradictory society halfway between capitalism and socialism, in which: (a) the productive forces are still far from adequate to give the state property a socialist character; (b) the tendency toward primitive accumulation created by want breaks out through innumerable pores of the planned economy; (c) norms of distribution preserving a bourgeois character lie at the basis of a new differentiation of society; (d) the economic growth, while slowly bettering the situation of the toilers, promotes a swift formation of privileged strata; (e) exploiting the social antagonisms, a bureaucracy has converted itself into an uncontrolled caste alien to socialism; (f) the social revolution, betrayed by the ruling party, still exists in property relations and in the consciousness of the toiling masses; (g) a further development of the accumulating contradictions can as well lead to socialism as back to capitalism; (h) on the road to capitalism the counterrevolution would have to break the resistance of the workers; (i) on the road to socialism the workers would have to overthrow

the bureaucracy. In the last analysis, the question will be decided by a struggle of living social forces, both on the national and the world arena.[18]

Bonapartism and the transitional regime

Trotsky sought to explain Stalin as part of a tyrannical lineage: Julius Caesar and Napoleon Bonaparte, as well as Napoleon's nephew Louis-Napoleon Bonaparte (who became Napoleon III). In each case, a somewhat similar governing system took the name of the individual in question. Caesarism, Bonapartism, Stalinism each involves the rise, in a strife torn society and highly factionalized political atmosphere, of an authoritarian 'super-arbiter' who utilizes democratic and popular rhetoric and claims to represent the interests of society as a whole. The power of the state is raised above the nation, apparently independent of all social classes, although actually preserving the privileges of the upper strata.

'The Stalin regime, rising above a politically atomized society, resting upon a police and officers' corps, and allowing of no control whatever, is obviously a variation of Bonapartism – a Bonapartism of a new type not before seen in history,' Trotsky wrote. 'Caesarism arose upon the basis of a slave society shaken by inward strife. Bonapartism is one of the political weapons of the capitalist regime in its critical period. Stalinism is a variety of the same system, but upon the basis of a workers' state torn by the antagonism between an organized and armed soviet aristocracy and the unarmed toiling masses.'[19]

Trotsky compared this with another form of 20th century Bonapartism – fascism. 'Stalinism and fascism, in spite of a deep difference in social foundations, are symmetrical phenomena,' he observed, adding: 'In many of their features they show a deadly similarity.' A revolutionary internationalist insight was also highlighted in his analysis: 'the crushing of Soviet democracy by an all-powerful bureaucracy and the extermination of bourgeois democracy by fascism were produced by one and the same cause: the dilatoriness of the world proletariat in solving the problems set for it by history.' Obviously thinking of the ongoing Spanish civil war and revolutionary possibilities in France, he added: 'A victorious revolutionary movement in Europe would immediately shake not only fascism, but Soviet Bonapartism.'[20]

Trotsky denied that the privileged Soviet bureaucracy actually constituted a class similar to the slave owning patricians, the feudal nobility, or the capitalist bourgeoisie. It did not represent either a variation of capitalism ('state capitalism') or a new form of class society (such as 'bureaucratic-collectivism'). Rather, he saw the Soviet bureaucracy as being akin to the enriched, conservative, undemocratic, and sometimes gangster-ridden bureaucratic layer that has so often arisen in the trade union movements of many countries. This parasitic elite, he felt, did not serve the same organic function as did the bourgeoisie in the capitalist mode of production. Therefore, the roots of the bureaucracy in Soviet society were not as deep, the bureaucratic stratum as a whole not as resilient, and the future of the bureaucracy as a ruling elite not able to be sustained as has been the case, for example, with the capitalist class.

The fact that the bureaucratic system consolidated under Stalin collapsed under the weight of its own contradictions after only six decades would seem to vindicate Trotsky's insistence that it does not represent a new form of class society. He saw bureaucratic rule not as a final resting-place for the revolutionary process in the USSR but, instead, as transitional. Yet he warned against 'the mistaken idea that from the present Soviet regime only a transition to socialism is possible. In reality a backslide to capitalism is wholly possible.' [21]

Contradictions and predictions

According to Trotsky, the growth and power of the bureaucracy came into conflict with a rationalization of the economy and the development of productive forces in the USSR. 'Just as absolute monarchy became in its time irreconcilable with the development of the bourgeois market,' capricious bureaucratic management (an essential element in Stalin's hyper-centralized 'command economy') prevented the keeping of accurate accounts essential for rational planning. Red tape, bottlenecks, nepotism, and incompetence in a relatively autonomous bureaucracy – free from the threat of controls imposed either by laws of the market or by workers' democracy – vastly complicated the tasks of economic production and distribution. Even with the meeting and surpassing of phenomenal production quotas, bureaucratically imposed from the top down, the quality of goods produced inevitably suffered. 'Bureaucratism destroys the creative initiative and the feeling of responsibility without which there is not, and cannot be qualitative progress.'[22]

The brunt of this is born by Soviet consumers. 'The ulcers of bureaucratism are perhaps not so obvious in the big industries,' Trotsky commented, 'but they are devouring, together with the co-operatives, the light and food-producing industries, the collective farms, the small local industries – that is, all those branches of economy which stand nearest to the people.' While 'it is possible to build gigantic factories according to a ready-made Western pattern by bureaucratic command – although, to be sure, at triple the normal cost,' this is not viable for long term economic development. 'The farther you go, the more the economy runs into the problem of quality, which slips out of the hands of a bureaucracy like a shadow.' Noting that 'Soviet products are as though branded with the grey label of indifference,' Trotsky also placed his finger on the alternative to the dictatorship of both the bureaucracy and the capitalist market: 'Under a nationalized economy, quality demands a democracy of producers and consumers, freedom of criticism and initiative – conditions incompatible with a totalitarian regime of fear, lies and flattery.... Soviet democracy is not the demand of an abstract policy, still less an abstract moral. It has become a life-and-death need of the country.'[23]

The contradictions of the Soviet economy – the gains of the October Revolution being continually undermined by the bureaucratic impact – asserted themselves throughout the existence of the Soviet Union, beautifully captured in the later formulation by Catherine Samary: 'full but bad employment; free services but of more and more disastrous quality; increases in education and skills, but without freedom of thought; and so on.'[24]

In the mid-1930s the Soviet bureaucracy, beset by intense internal and external pressures, stood at a crossroads. A portion of it reflected an inclination to move in the direction of 'liberal' reform. But the very thought of this was soon obliterated by the assassination of Leningrad party boss Sergei Kirov, in retrospect sometimes seen as Stalin's potential rival, yet identified by more recent historians as a firm 'Stalin man.' Kirov's murder was used as a pretext for the mass arrests, imprisonment, and slaughter of real, potential, and imagined opponents of Stalin's regime – all accused of being part of a 'counterrevolutionary Trotskyite conspiracy.'[25]

Trotsky's analysis was completed just as this living nightmare began. Yet he considered what might happen if, on the contrary, a 'liberal reform' wing of the bureaucracy made headway. Predicting that economic crisis would generate 'an open political crisis,' he suggested that, as a preventive measure, the new Soviet constitution of 1936 might be utilized to channel deep popular discontent into the voting booth in order to admonish and correct sectors of the bureaucracy responsible for some of the society's difficulties. 'However, it has happened more than once that a bureaucratic dictatorship, seeking salvation in "liberal" reforms, has only weakened itself,' Trotsky wrote, pointing out that this could create 'a semilegal cover for the struggle against' the regime. Trotsky predicted: 'The rivalry of bureaucratic cliques at the elections may become the beginning of a broader political struggle. The whip against "badly working organs of power" may be turned into a whip against Bonapartism.' What failed to mature in the 1930s became the reality half a century later: 'All indications agree that the further course of development must inevitably lead to a clash between the culturally developed forces of the people and the bureaucratic oligarchy.... With energetic pressure from the popular mass, and the disintegration inevitable in such circumstances of the government apparatus, the resistance of those in power may prove much weaker than now appears.'[26]

Trotsky did not assume that only good things could result. He favoured a political revolution, renewing Soviet democracy, and leaving the socio-economic conquests of the 1917 revolution intact and deepening them. But he was able to envision a grim alternate scenario:

> *A collapse of the Soviet regime would lead inevitably to the collapse of the planned economy, and thus to the abolition of state property. The bond of compulsion between the trusts and the factories within them would fall away. The more successful enterprises would succeed in coming out on the road of independence. They might convert themselves into stock companies, or they might find some other transitional form of property – one, for example, in which the workers should participate in the profits. The collective farms would disintegrate at the same time, and far more easily. The fall of the present bureaucratic dictatorship, if it were not replaced by a new socialist power, would thus mean a return to capitalist relations with a catastrophic decline of industry and culture.*[27]

Bad as daily life under Stalinist tyranny might be, things could get worse. The job security could be replaced with the economic whip of unemployment. There could be the erosion of housing, medical care, education, and other social benefits guaranteed by the 1917 revolution. 'The vast majority of the Soviet workers are even now hostile to the bureaucracy,' Trotsky argued, but 'the workers have almost never come out on the road of open struggle,' because of the fear that, 'in throwing out the bureaucracy, they will open the way for a capitalist restoration.' Trotsky saw this as a dialectical contradiction in the Soviet reality. The destruction of the planned economy would set the country back for decades, so the bureaucracy fulfilled a necessary function by preserving that economy. 'But it fulfils it in such a way as to prepare an explosion of the whole system which may completely sweep out the results of the revolution.'[28]

Whether the USSR would finally slide back into capitalism or move forward to socialism would be resolved through immense struggles involving the Soviet masses themselves.

This opinion that Trotsky expressed more than once is consistent with a point that Ernest Mandel would express in later years, often in his characteristic spirit of boundless optimism. There was however an essential element in Trotsky's analysis which is too often overlooked.

The importance of the Left Opposition

Trotsky knew that relatively spontaneous mass upsurges of the working class could *begin* a revolution, but he did not believe this meant the working class could 'spontaneously' *win* a revolution. Taking political power was possible only through conscious preparation, including the development of experienced militants, as well as the development of a sound political program and the ability to effectively communicate it to masses of people. He believed the existence of the Left Opposition in the USSR – which at that time he considered the largest section of the Fourth International – constituted such a force.

This was by no means a figment of his imagination. These courageous men and women – in many cases veterans of the revolutionary struggle against tsarism and capitalism, leading cadres in the 1917 revolution and the civil war period, early defenders of Marxism and Bolshevik principles against the first signs of bureaucratic corruption – constituted a tremendous reservoir of political experience, organizing skill, and invaluable moral authority.[29]

'The prisons, the remote comers of Siberia and Central Asia, the fast-multiplying concentration camps, contain the flower of the Bolshevik Party, the most sturdy and true,' Trotsky wrote. Acknowledging the loss of hundreds of Left Oppositionists through executions, starvation during hunger strikes, suicides, etc., he stated that at least 20,000 remained. The Communist Party of Stalin had two million, but 'on such a question a mere juxtaposition of figures means nothing,' Trotsky pointed out. 'Ten revolutionists in a regiment is enough to bring it over, in a red-hot political atmosphere, to the side of the people.'[30] He quoted the recently freed Victor Serge, one of the few Left Oppositionists to escape from the prison camps:

> *Thousands of these Communists of the first hour, comrades of Lenin and Trotsky, builders of the Soviet Republic when Soviets still existed, are opposing the principles of socialism to the inner degeneration of the regime, are defending as best they can (and all they can is to agree to all possible sacrifices) the rights of the working class .... I bring you news of those who are locked up there. They will hold out, whatever be necessary, to the end. Even if they do not live to see a new revolutionary dawn.*[31]

One of the most important changes to take place since Trotsky wrote *The Revolution Betrayed* is that these comrades – precious human beings, irreplaceable revolutionary cadres – were almost completely eliminated. Some were finally broken, capitulating to Stalin's authority. Others were able to stand fast to their beliefs, and they were massacred in 1937-38. There are accounts of them being marched out in batches from the labour camps, at gunpoint, into the tundra. Some eyewitnesses recount that they walked with dignity, raising the Communist clenched-fist salute, and proudly, defiantly sang 'The Internationale' before reaching the spot where they were shot down.

Vision of socialist renewal

It can be argued, however, that the historic program of the Left Opposition remains vibrant as a socialist vision. 'The restoration of democracy in the trade unions and the Soviets ... would be able to, and would have to, restore freedom of Soviet parties.... A restoration of the right of criticism, and a genuine freedom of elections, are necessary conditions for the further development of the country.' Trotsky had no patience for the anxiety that some might stumble into political 'heresy' and error. 'The youth will receive the opportunity to breathe freely, criticize, make mistakes, and grow up. Science and art will be freed of their chains.'[32]

There would be a settling of accounts, a necessary cleansing. 'Together with the masses, and at their head, [a revolutionary party] would carry out a ruthless purgation of the state apparatus,' eliminating the tyranny of Stalinism root and branch. Of course, 'it is not a question of substituting one ruling clique for another, but of changing the very methods of administering the economy and guiding the culture of the country. Bureaucratic autocracy must give place to Soviet democracy.'[33]

Ending the bureaucratic strangulation of the means of production and distribution, 'the proletariat would have to introduce in the economy a series of very important reforms, but not another social revolution.' Rather, 'it would retain and further develop the experiment of planned economy.'[34]

But the planning must assume a qualitatively different character: 'The bringing of democracy into industry means a radical revision of plans in the interests of the toilers. Free discussion of economic problems will decrease the overhead expense of bureaucratic mistakes and zig-zags. ... 'Bourgeois norms of distribution [such as inequality of incomes, market mechanisms, etc.] will be confined within the limits of strict necessity, and, in step with the growth of social wealth, will give way to socialist equality.'[35]

'And, finally,' Trotsky concluded, 'foreign policy will return to the traditions of revolutionary internationalism.' Insisting on the utter utopianism of the Stalinist notion of building socialism in a single country, he warned: 'The longer the Soviet Union remains in a capitalist environment, the deeper runs the degeneration of the social fabric. A prolonged isolation would inevitably end not in national communism, but in a restoration of capitalism.' He added: 'If a bourgeoisie cannot peacefully grow into a socialist democracy, it is likewise true that a socialist state cannot peacefully merge with a world capitalist system.' The Bolsheviks, upon taking power in 1917, had proclaimed their 'fundamental task' to be 'the establishment of a socialist organization of society and the victory of socialism in all countries.' This must guide a revitalized Soviet Union, Trotsky insisted. 'More than ever the fate of the October revolution is bound up now with the fate of Europe and of the whole world.'[36]

Trotsky did not believe bureaucratic tyranny in the Soviet Union would be capable of enduring for another half century. From the horrors and carnage of the Second World War, and in reaction against what the various capitalist regimes and the Stalin regime had done to the world – Trotsky believed – a revolutionary wave would sweep across the planet and bring into being a socialist world. This was reflected in the 1938 founding manifesto of the Fourth International: 'The advanced workers, united in the Fourth International, show their class the way out of the crisis.... Workers – men and women – of all countries, place yourselves under the banner of the Fourth International. It is the banner of your approaching victory.'[37]

The fact that the anticipated revolutionary triumph was not forthcoming resulted in crisis and fissures in the small but vibrant revolutionary movement inspired by Trotsky's perspectives. He himself had been assassinated as the war began to unfold, so it was left to his contending comrades to try to make sense of the realities they faced. A manifestation of the resulting divergences is the Mandel-Harman debate.

II. Reflections on the state capitalism debate – and beyond

Mandel and Harman quite clearly state their own cases, and each reader will have to judge who seems to have a better grasp of the complexities discussed. My concluding comments will be restricted to (1) a historiographic matter relevant to the debate, (2) what strike me as strengths in Mandel's contribution, and (3) some critical thoughts on aspects of Mandel's perspectives.

Suggestive for discussions and debates regarding the notion of *state capitalism*, it seems to me, is Jürgen Kocka's succinct but ambitious historical survey of capitalism. 'Early rudiments' of capitalism, he tells us, have existed *throughout the world* for thousands of years, reflected in the creation of commodities, the existence of currency, trade routes, commercial transactions, and more. These can be found in Imperial China, in what is now India, in the Middle East, in portions of Africa, in the Roman Empire, etc., blending with other, more dominant economic systems over the centuries.[38]

According to Kocka, a mature capitalist system came into being in Europe through a process taking place between 1500 and 1800 – crystallizing, essentially, as the dominant mode of production (drawing more and more aspects of life into a system of generalized commodity production, driven by a relentless capital accumulation process) within more and more areas of our planet down to the present-day. As it has done so, Kocka tells us, it has assumed various forms that include merchant capitalism, plantation capitalism, industrial capitalism, and finance capitalism.[39]

One can best comprehend capitalism as an incredibly dynamic *process of development*, a process of capital accumulation, transforming the world over and over again. This complex and dynamically evolving reality, a vast and contradictory process, assumes different forms in different moments of history and in different places on our planet. The diversity of 'capitalisms' cannot be defined by a single description.[40]

This would seem to harmonize with capitalist elements of economic life in the Soviet Union discussed by Chris Harman and his co-thinkers in a way that supports their theory – the existence of *a diversity of capitalisms* would certainly seem to leave room for their notion of 'state capitalism.'

There remains, however, Mandel's insistence that the dynamics of the Soviet economy were qualitatively different from those of what we generally understand as modern capitalist economies. The *capital accumulation process* was central to the system analysed by Marx, and Harman makes liberal use of the term in his own discussion of Soviet realities – but Mandel observes that it seems to have a different meaning in Harman's analysis.

The Soviet economy and 'traditional' capitalist economies also seem to function differently in regard to the 'law of value' and the tendency toward overproduction – according to Mandel each economic system operates according to a different logic (or illogic). Far more than shedding light on the economic system dominant in the Soviet Union, he stresses, the state capitalism concept blunts one's understanding of the capitalism that came into being in the Modern Era and has been evolving since then into the global system that dominates our lives. Kocka may identify capitalist 'rudiments' in Imperial China or the Roman Empire, but this hardly means they each constitute a variant of capitalism.

A key element in the analysis advanced by Harman and others sharing Tony Cliff's analysis is that the capitalist world market creates the essential context within which to understand the dynamics of the state capitalist system of the USSR. It is this which results in the capitalist law of value being a central element in the Soviet economy. According to Mandel, the reverse is true. He points out that the nature of Soviet industry (highly 'unproductive' and therefore unprofitable and uncompetitive from a capitalist standpoint) caused the ruling bureaucracy to shield at least two-thirds of Soviet enterprises from competition with the highly productive firms of capitalism's global market.[41]

Mandel goes on to note that – with 'the collapse of Communism' – assertions about state capitalism seem to pale: 'Now, as has been clear for a long time, the issue is posed whether capitalism will be restored in Eastern Europe, the Soviet Union, Cuba and China.' If such countries were already capitalist, what would there be to restore? Despite bureaucratic degeneration or deformities, revolutionary gains (the 'gains of October' that Trotsky insisted must be defended) would seem to have been real after all, targeted by bureaucrats transforming themselves into entrepreneurial oligarchs. As Mandel puts it:

Socialists must resist every attempt to destroy the collectivized property relation – concretely this means battling without reservation against attempts to privatize enterprises and destroy the social gains of the working class – the inefficient, unfair, chronically disorganized, but nonetheless real gains of huge subsidies on rents and food, ultra-cheap housing and transport, free childcare and healthcare – and above all guaranteed employment.

Mandel seems to offer a reasonable program here, one consistent with the underlying analysis he advances. (It should be noted that in his final essay in this volume, Harman concurs with the need to resist privatization – which seems inconsistent, however, with his own underlying analysis.) Those who read these polemics will need to determine the extent to which Mandel's side of this debate, and that of his adversary, make sense. Yet such matters continue to have more than simply theoretical importance in our ever-changing world – with profound implications for today. This is certainly the case in regard to Cuba, a country very much within Mandel's purview in yet earlier debates with Harman.[42] It is quite likely that other situations will arise in coming years that highlight the debate's continuing relevance.

It would be contrary to the Marxist method, however, to imagine that Mandel's contributions here close the book on what is true and what is not. The ongoing processes of social reality require that we approach any such contributions with critical minds. Some of what played out in the years after the final polemic in this volume indicates a profound disconnect between an essential element in Mandel's theoretical perspective and the realities of Soviet life. This does not come to the fore in the polemics of this volume, but it did later, and it has implications for what Mandel argues and fails to argue in these pages.

In his 1989 book *Beyond Perestroika*, Mandel took issue with the widespread belief in the inability of 'the Soviet masses to intervene in political life in an autonomous fashion.' He explained: 'The existence now in Soviet society of a proletarian majority which is educated and qualified and irresistibly drawn towards self-activity, at least on the enterprise level, creates for the first time a potential force capable of ridding the Soviet Union of its bureaucratic heap.' Ten years earlier, he had emphasized that the Soviet working class, while disappointed that the October Revolution had degenerated in a way that did not meet their needs, had 'not been attracted to the capitalist model either,' and that the restoration of capitalism in the Soviet Union through some kind of 'palace revolution' was impossible – 'the restoration of capitalism could only occur through new and disastrous defeats of the Soviet and international proletariat, through violent political and social upheavals.' In the new situation of 1989, he explained, 'the prediction made by Leon Trotsky half a century ago has turned out to be more realistic and more probable.' Mandel then offered a long quotation from Trotsky explaining what a political revolution by the Soviet working class would accomplish, concluding his book with the words: 'That is how it will be.'[43]

Of course, that is not how it was. 'The class consequences for the "transitional society" of a crystallized bureaucratization were that it really blocked any development towards social-ism,' Catherine Samary has aptly noted. Consequently, she stresses, 'Mandel should have stressed that *the anti-worker content of the Soviet state was dominant*, both weakening the workers' capacity to resist capitalist restoration and favour-ing a bureaucratic turn towards capitalism.' She goes on to suggest that preventing the return of capitalism would have required not simply the traditionally sanctioned *political revo-lution*. 'A social revolution was still needed.' [44]

This opens an important area for further analytical explora-tion, discussion and debate.

But there seems to me an additional gap in Mandel's anal-ysis, involving the dialectical interplay between (1) the time it takes to develop what is sometimes called a 'revolutionary vanguard' and (2) the time it takes for such vanguard sectors of the working class to help the working class as a whole develop sufficient class consciousness and political experience to bring about a revolutionary overturn. A careful examination of Trotsky's *Revolution Betrayed* reveals a belief that the possibility of a political revolution in the Soviet Union, and of the forward movement toward socialism, was dependent not simply on the size and desires and educational level of the Soviet working class. A central element in Trotsky's analysis involved the contin-ued existence and the role to be played by the experienced cadres of the Left Opposition. This is related to his own expe-rience in the decades leading up to the Russian Revolution of 1917. There was a process of at least ten to twenty years within which organizations of seasoned cadres formed and functioned as an indispensable revolutionary leaven within the working class, culminating in the triumph of 1917.[45]

In 1985, the *Glasnost* of the Gorbachev period opened up the freedom for such developments to begin. But they had hardly advanced sufficiently to justify Mandel's 1989 certainties about the immanent working-class socialist triumph. In Mandel's other writings one finds a mixed record on such matters. His buoyant optimism may sometimes have caused him to assume more from reality than it could deliver, yet more measured formulations strike a better balance in key documents.[46]

Mandel's polemics in the present volume may not provide a finished understanding of the vast and complex realities with which he is wrestling. Some contributions in our earlier volume of his writings (not least being 'The Leninist Theory of Organization') provide elements for further developing the analyses presented here. More than this, he would be the first to insist that one must look beyond his own works to overcome inevitable limitations in what he might offer. This would mean considering what others have to say, studying the further unfolding of economic, political and social realities, and learning from the experience of actual struggles. At the same time, engagement with what Ernest Mandel offers can provide not only theoretical insights, but also ideas that might help advance the struggle for human liberation.

Introduction to *Fallacies of state capitalism*

Phil Hearse

More than twenty years ago, Ernest Mandel, Chris Harman and Michael Kidron debated the issue of the class nature of the Soviet Union in a polemic, which has been reprinted many times. In the summer of 1990, this debate was re-joined, when Chris Harman published a long critique of Mandel's book *Beyond Perestroika* in the pages of *International Socialism*. We are publishing here the exchange which followed.[47]

Most socialists in Britain, where the far left has been dominated by the Trotskyist tradition, will be familiar with the general lines of the debate on the USSR. Starting with Trotsky's analysis of the Soviet bureaucracy, three main theoretical frameworks to explain the USSR emerged – the 'transitional society' or 'degenerated workers' state' theory; the theory of bureaucratic state capitalism associated with Tony Cliff; and the 'bureaucratic collectivism' theory associated initially with writers like James Burnham, Max Shachtman and Bruno Rizzi.

Since this debate, in one form or another, has raged for more than 50 years, many socialists are inclined to consider it an irrelevance or, at best, a secondary matter. But the protagonists in the current debate do not, and in our view rightly. Clearly, the huge developments in the Soviet Union put in question the social order which has existed since the counter-revolutionary victory of Stalinism in the late 1920s and early 1930s. Obviously this has a massive impact on world politics. Socialists are bound to return to fundamental theories to analyse not just the historical question of 'what went wrong' in the Soviet Union, but also contemporary questions of what is happening in the USSR, and thus what the tasks of socialists worldwide are.

The debate assumes particular acuteness in Britain, where the Socialist Workers Party (SWP) insists that only the theory of state capitalism has any explanatory power in relation to the fiasco of *Perestroika*, and indeed that other theories of the USSR lead their supporters, consciously or otherwise, to 'capitulate to Stalinism'.

Thus, the SWP insist that only revolutionary organizations built on the basis of the theory of state capitalism can adequately meet the needs of today's political situation. And thus, they have insisted on trying to build small organizations internationally which agree totally with the SWP on this question.

The view that revolutionary organizations must be built on the basis of this or that *theory* of the Soviet Union has never been the attitude of the Fourth International (FI). Revolutionary organizations are built on the basis of common *programme*, which implies at least a minimum threshold of agreement on current tasks.

This was the attitude of Trotsky, when his degenerated workers' state theory was first put in question inside the FI. In a famous letter to Shachtman published in *In Defence of Marxism* Trotsky asks what *programmatic* consequences a different theory of the Soviet Union implies. If there are none, he insists, then there is no basis for a split.

To what extent are there major programmatic differences between the FI and the SWP on this question today? Evidently, there is one huge difference of analysis. For the SWP the restoration of capitalism in the USSR merely be a 'step sideways' since for them it is just the replacement of one form of capitalism by another. Logically, they would argue that capitalist restoration should not be opposed; but in practice, whatever one thinks of their reasoning, the SWP insist they are indeed opposed to privatisation of enterprises, which is necessarily a central aspect of capitalist restoration.

For the FI on the other hand, the restoration of capitalism means a major defeat for the working class internationally. In our view, at this stage, despite the differences of analysis, the position of the SWP on capitalist restoration is at best dangerously ambiguous. Both the FI and the SWP declare for independent trade unions, a new revolutionary socialist party, for the overthrow of the bureaucracy. If on the other hand, the SWP insist that a new party must be based solely on the theory of state capitalism, and that opposition to capitalist restoration is not a central task for it, then major differences remain.

In any case, the differences between the SWP and the FI, especially in Britain, go way beyond analysis of the Soviet Union. Central disputes revolve around the character of the revolutionary party which needs to be built, orientation to the mass organizations of the working class, the role of the movements of the specially oppressed and the international organization of revolutionaries.

Revolutionaries in both the SWP and the Fourth International nonetheless have to face realities. The Fourth International remains the most important international regroupment of revolutionary socialist forces; it will not go away. But neither will the SWP, which has built itself in Britain into a significant organization, which although still small in relation to the mass revolutionary party which needs to be built, nonetheless has several thousand members. Since the late 1970s discussion between the FI and the SWP has been extremely limited. It is high time that this discussion was renewed. But to be of value it must go beyond the rehearsal of theoretical differences over state capitalism. In both Chris Harman's 'A theory which does not withstand the test of logic' and Mandel's final article, the more immediately political differences between the two organizations begin to be addressed. This is a promising step forward.

The semi-collapse of Stalinism in Eastern Europe has engendered a major offensive by the right-wing internationally, proclaiming a 'crisis of socialism' and the end of the tradition opened up by the October revolution. Marxists are duty bound to answer this debate, not just by defence of the anti-Stalinist Marxist tradition – vital though that is – but by demonstrating the validity of their programme and concrete political answers.

The idea that this can happen by the simple reiteration of the tradition of this or that small Marxist tendency is bankrupt. A new dialogue, a new clarification of the tasks of building an international revolutionary movement, is needed. This current discussion can help to begin that process.

Phil Hearse
November 1991

From Trotsky to state capitalism

Chris Harman

The USSR today displays all the symptoms of a society entering a prolonged period of social and political turmoil. Such periods always represent a great challenge but also offer great opportunities to the revolutionary left internationally. But to meet them the left has to have a clear understanding of what is happening and why. It has to have a revolutionary theory to guide its revolutionary practice.

There are a number of different theoretical analyses of the USSR on the revolutionary left. Ernest Mandel is one of the best-known proponents of the theory that sees it as a degenerated workers' state, Tony Cliff of the theory that sees it as bureaucratic state capitalist. The appearance in the last few months of Mandel's book *Beyond Perestroika* in an English translation and of Tony Cliff's *State Capitalism in Russia* in French translation offers the opportunity to contrast the two analyses and to see which best comes to terms with current realities.

Both Mandel and Cliff come from the Trotskyist tradition. Cliff was a member of the Fourth International in Palestine and Britain during the 1930s and 1940s before playing a leading role in the Socialist Workers Party of Britain (previously the

International Socialists), of which he is still a leading activist. Mandel has been a leading figure in the Fourth International since the mid 1940s.

Both started off by accepting the same analysis of Russia, that elaborated by Trotsky in the 1930s. But in the late 1940's developments in Eastern Europe led to a period of intense discussion in the international Trotskyist movement which drew Cliff and Mandel in different theoretical directions.

Trotsky had argued in the 1930s that the bureaucracy in the USSR was a 'caste.' It was a stratum of society which had been able to take advantage of the isolation of the Russian Revolution (to which it then contributed!), the poverty of the country and the weariness of the masses to concentrate power and privilege in its own hands. But it was only able to do so by balancing between the working class and bourgeois and petty bourgeois forces at home and internationally:

> *The Soviet (it would be more accurate to say, the anti-Soviet) bureaucratism is the product of the social contradiction between the city and the village; between the proletariat and the peasantry; between the national republics and districts; between the different groups of peasantry; between the different layers of the working class; between the different groups of consumers; and finally between the Soviet state and its capitalist environment ...Rising above the toiling masses, the bureaucracy regulates all these contradictions ...*[48]

It was 'not an independent class but an excrescence upon the proletariat.'[49] To this extent it could be compared with the trade union bureaucracy in the West: it betrayed the working class, it used the working class for its own ends, but was still to some degree dependent on the working class. It did not have its own independent roots in the ownership of property or in production, but was a parasitic outgrowth based on contradictions in the realm of consumption. As such it impeded the development of society, without substituting any new development Trent based on its own class interests.

'A tumour can grow to a tremendous size and even strangle the living organism, but a tumour can never become an independent organism.'[50]

Because of this, it served to retard the development of the country. 'The further unhindered development of bureaucratism must lead inevitably to the cessation of economic and cultural growth, to a terrible social crisis, and to the downward plunge of the entire society.'[51]

In his early formulations of the analysis Trotsky drew the conclusion that the bureaucracy could still be brought to order peacefully by a resurgent working class:

> *The recognition of the present Soviet state as a workers' state not only signifies that the bourgeoisie can conquer power only by means of an armed uprising, but also that the proletariat of the USSR has not forfeited the possibility of subordinating the bourgeoisie to it, of reviving the party again, and of regenerating the regime of the dictatorship – without a new revolution, with the methods and on the road to reform.*[52]

But he was not afraid to change his account in the light of the harsh experience of what Stalinism in power meant. In October 1933 he wrote, 'The bureaucracy can be compelled to yield power into the hands of the proletarian vanguard only by force.'[53]

The Revolution Betrayed, written three years later, was absolutely adamant that it was not possible to reform either the party or the state:

> *All indications agree that the further course of development must inevitably lead to a clash between the culturally developed forces of the people and the bureaucratic oligarchy. There is no peaceful outcome to this crisis. No devil has ever cut off his own claw. The Soviet bureaucracy will not give up its positions without a fight. The development obviously leads to the road of revolution.*[54]

This revolution, he argued, was a 'political' not a social revolution, although it would be a political revolution with 'deep social consequences.'[55]

Trotsky's attitude to the bureaucracy hardened even more in the last four years before he was murdered. He insisted that it was a counter-revolutionary force, a product of the pressure of the bourgeoisie on the working class. But he still insisted it was a not a class. Powerful sections of the bureaucracy wanted to turn themselves into a class, but they could only do so by establishing private property of industry – and fear of the working class stopped them doing so. 'It [the bureaucracy] only preserves state property to the extent that it fears the proletariat ...'[56]

Just as the working class could not establish a healthy workers' state without revolution, the bureaucracy could not establish itself as a ruling class without a full-blooded counter-revolution. The bureaucracy seemed very powerful, Trotsky argued. But in reality its power could not last for long, 'Bonapartism by its very essence cannot long sustain itself: a sphere balanced on the point of a pyramid must invariably roll down on one side or the other.'[57]

One of his arguments against the 'new class theory' developed by Shachtman and others in 1939 was that as revolutionary socialists we would 'place ourselves in a ludicrous position if we fixed to the Bonapartist oligarchy the nomenclature of a new ruling class just a few years or even a few months before its inglorious downfall.'[58]

In 1940 he spelt out the argument even more forcefully. The outbreak of war would constitute an increase in all the contradictory pressures within the USSR and there would be no chance of the bureaucracy being able to continue its balancing act. 'In case of a protracted war accompanied by the passivity of the world proletariat the internal contradictions in the USSR not only might but would have to lead to a bourgeois-Bonapartist counter-revolution.'[59]

The problem Trotsky's followers had to face after the war was that, far from falling apart or even weakening, the Stalinist bureaucracy was stronger than ever. Its armies had extended the boundaries of the USSR and had established regimes virtually identical to the USSR in Eastern Europe – a feat soon to be copied by Mao Zedong's army in China. If the USSR was a degenerated workers' state, then logically these regimes must be some form of workers' state as well. But what then happened to Trotsky's contentions that the Stalinist bureaucracy was 'counter-revolutionary' – or to the general Marxist contention that revolution from below was needed to destroy capitalism?

The revolutionaries of the Fourth International wrestled with these contradictions in Trotsky's analysis through 1947–9. Some (including both Cliff and Mandel briefly) attempted to fit the facts into the old analysis: Russia was a degenerated workers' state, but the Eastern European states bourgeois dictatorships (a position still ostensibly held by *Lutte Ouvrière* in France). But soon two positions crystallized, both in their own way different to Trotsky's.

The first was to use much of the phraseology of Trotsky's formulations, but to accept that Stalinism could be a revolutionary force despite itself, and to proclaim the East European states 'deformed workers' states.' This was the position taken by Mandel, Pierre Frank, Michel Pablo and others.

It was this path which led some people very easily away from the spirit of Trotsky's theory. Pablo, for instance, concluded that if the Stalinist parties could be revolutionary, then humanity faced 'hundreds of years of deformed workers' states' and the job of revolutionaries was to help in their creation by entering the Stalinist parties.[60] Meanwhile, Isaac Deutscher, a pre-war Trotskyist who had opposed the formation of the Fourth International, argued that the growth of industry inside the USSR would automatically lead Stalinism to reform itself. Again, the logic was to abandon independent revolutionary politics. Deutscher wrote in 1953 that 'the effect of the Berlin revolt was objectively counter-revolutionary and not revolutionary' because it had contributed to 'Beria's downfall' at a time when 'Beria was one of those who stood for democratic reform.'[61] He later transferred his trust to Khrushchev, writing of the uprisings of the 1950s that:

> *Eastern Europe (Hungary, Poland, and East Germany)
> ... found itself on the brink of bourgeois restoration at the
> end of the Stalin era; and only Soviet armed power (or its
> threat) stopped it there.*[62]

Meanwhile, a section of Pablo's supporters backed the crushing of the Hungarian revolution by Russian troops. Of course, such people weren't necessarily uncritical of Stalinism or of Khrushchev. Right to the end of his life in 1968 Deutscher continued to argue for a democratic version of socialism. But the important point was that he saw the Russian bureaucracy, acting from above, as an agent that could take us part of the way there.

The mainstream of the Fourth International managed to avoid such extreme conclusions. But they did tend to see the Russian bloc as a progressive historical force. Mandel, for example, would argue that the growth rate of the Russian economy alone was enough to demonstrate the superiority of its economy over any of capitalism (forgetting Trotsky's prognosis nearly 20 years before of the imminent collapse of that economy!):

> *The Soviet Union maintains a more or less even rhythm of
> economic growth, plan after plan, decade after decade,
> without the progress of the past weighing on the possi-
> bilities of the future ... All the laws of development of
> the capitalist economy which provoke a slowdown in the
> speed of economic growth are eliminated.*[63]

And if Mandel never made Deutscher's mistake of opposing the risings of 1953 in East Germany and 1956 in Hungary, he did tend to identify reform from above in Eastern Europe with the 'political revolution.' So he expressed a clear preference in 1956 for the methods of Gomulka in Warsaw to those of the revolutionaries in Budapest. He could write that, although 'socialist democracy will still have many battles to win in Poland, the principal battle, that which has permitted millions of workers to identify themselves again with the workers' state, is already won.'[64]

This trend is continued today by many people who claim to base themselves on Trotsky's analysis. Thus, for instance, Tariq Ali – who says his 'political formation' was 'greatly influenced by Isaac Deutscher, Leon Trotsky and Ernest Mandel (in that order)' – puts enormous faith in Gorbachev in his aptly titled book *Revolution from Above*. 'In order to preserve the Soviet Union', he writes, 'Gorbachev needs to complete the political revolution which is already underway.'

Fortunately, the tone of Mandel's book on *Perestroika* is different. He tells us:

> *Gorbachev represents the response of the modernist wing of the bureaucracy to the threat to the stability of its rule represented by this crisis [of the Soviet system] and by the rise of public awareness. To channel these changes and to try to keep them under the bureaucracy's control – this is the historic project of the Gorbachev wing of the Soviet bureaucracy.*[65]
>
> *Underlying the apparent realism of Gorbachev is a profoundly conservative vision of reality, which corresponds perfectly to the social and ideological conservatism of the Soviet bureaucracy ...*[66]

Mandel argues strongly against those who say what is taking place today is 'a revolution from above':

> *The point of the exercise is to prevent a revolutionary explosion, in other words, a 'revolution from below.' But, for this very reason, these measures are radical reforms and not revolution in the proper sense of the word ...*[67]

Yet the tone is not always so sure, as when he writes that 'the only valid verdict' on measures taken by Gorbachev 'is a nuanced one, case by case, problem by problem ... Too bad for the over simplifiers.'[68] It is as if Mandel, having taken a sharp turn against those like Tariq Ali, who would have us put our trust in Gorbachev, is still not fully convinced that they are wrong.

But if Mandel's conclusions are not fully coherent, the analysis on which he bases them is even less so. It is not just that the book contains an infuriating number of elementary factual errors.[69] More importantly, the theoretical underpinning of the argument is fundamentally flawed.

The most basic problem with the analysis concerns Mandel's understanding of the bureaucracy. He insists that the bureaucracy is not a class: 'The *nomenklatura* is not a ruling class but a fraction of a class which has usurped power from the working class ...'[70]

This leads him into all sorts of contradictions. He writes that 'the bureaucratic layer monopolises political power just as it does economic power'[71] and that 'the interests of the mass of producers, the workers and peasants ... are opposed to those of the directors/managers ...'[72]

He applies to it what he calls 'the essential law which emerges from the history of different societies', that 'the social group (social class or major section of a social class) which controls the social surplus because of its place in the production process, controls to a large extent all other activities too.'[73] It follows from 'the materialist interpretation of history' that:

> *Relations of domination flow from relations of production. These relations of domination cannot, except during brief periods of dual power, be in fundamental opposition to the relations of production.*

But if the bureaucracy 'controls the social surplus' because of 'its role in the production process', then 'its role' involves it exploiting the direct producers. And a 'group' which exploits the direct producers is, by definition, an exploiting class.

Of course, there have been many cases historically when a section of an exploiting class has concentrated power into its own hands and, thereby, creamed off much of the surplus previously disposed of by other sections of the ruling class. This was true, for instance, of the late feudal monarchy and, according to Marx, of the regimes of both Louis Philippe and Louis Bonaparte. But in these cases the surplus came, in the first place, from the class exploitation of the direct producers. The 'section of the class' was a section of an *exploiting* class.

It is a complete travesty of Marxism to claim that a section of the working class, i.e. of an *exploited* class, can control the surplus from exploitation. But Mandel does not pursue this line of argument. Three pages after putting it, he denies his own argument:

> *Unlike a real ruling class, the bureaucracy is unable to base its material privileges on the coherent functioning (i.e.,the reproduction) of the economic system, of its role in the production process ...*[74]

So on one page the bureaucracy 'controls the social surplus' because of 'its role in production.' Three pages later 'its material privileges', which presumably are part of the surplus, do not come from 'its role in the production process.' The confusion of the whole argument is increased still further when we are told later, 'In reality, a socialist society, a society without classes, does not exist in the USSR.'[75]

This confusion over whether the bureaucracy is a ruling class is part of a wider confusion. In Mandel's account there is no explanation of the dynamic of the Russian economy. Mandel, as we have seen, used to hold the view that planning made the Russian economy able to expand indefinitely. Now empirical reality has made him change his mind. He talks of economic 'crisis', and says, 'The most striking manifestation of this crisis is the slowdown in the rate of economic growth.'[76]

He explains this in three ways.

Mandel argues:

> *The contradictory development of Soviet society is precisely a product of the combination of dynamism and immobility. The dynamism results from economic and social growth (a product of what remains of the October revolution) which is impressive in the long term, even if it is slowing down year by year. The immobility results from the bureaucratic stranglehold on the state and society as a whole. This is an obstacle to further growth.*[77]

Elsewhere he makes the same point in a slightly different way:

> *The dominant layer in society seems incapable of develop-*
> *ing the system.*[78]

> *... the material interests of the bureaucracy [are] the prin-*
> *cipal, if not the only, motor force of plan fulfilment, of the*
> *daily functioning of the system. This robs the entire econ-*
> *omy of any form of economic rationality. The material inter-*
> *ests of the bureaucracy push in the direction of increasing*
> *access of goods and services to the bureaucracy itself and*
> *not in the direction of optimising the output of enterprises*
> *– and certainly not in the direction of maximising the rate*
> *of accumulation.*[79]

He goes on to argue:

> *Technically the fall in the growth rate expresses the regular*
> *increase in what, in the capitalist economy, we would call*
> *the 'capital coefficient.' The investment mass necessary to*
> *increase the national income by 1 per cent increases from*
> *one five-year plan to the next.*[80]

Finally, Mandel claims:

> *The plan/market relations, or what amounts to the same*
> *thing, the bureaucratic despotism/law of value relation ...*
> *[is] the fundamental contradiction of the economy ...*[81]

Let's look at each in turn.

In his first point Mandel's talk of a 'combination of dynamism and immobility' only makes sense if what is meant is that
the economy used to seem very dynamic, with growth rates
higher than most advanced Western countries (although not
all: Japan has probably done better on average), but that it is
increasingly prone to stagnation. But it is completely miscon-
ceived to try to explain the dynamism by 'what remains of the
October revolution' and the stagnation by the 'bureaucratic

stranglehold.' Such an explanation implies that the 'bureaucratic stranglehold' was less and the 'remains of the October revolution' greater at the time of the Moscow trials and the five to ten million slave labourers than today.

In fact, as every serious study of the five-year plans and industrialisation has shown, the drive to industrialisation and collective agriculture was carried through by the Stalin wing of the bureaucracy (assisted, it is true, by ex-Zinovievites, capitulationist left oppositionists like Preobrazhensky and Radek and the great mass of repentant Bukharinites). It came after what has sometimes been called 'the Stalin revolution' – the final and complete bureaucratization of the party, the state machine and the trade unions, and the use of the GPU to obliterate every expression of opposition.[82]

This bureaucratization did not simply, or even mainly, lead 'in the direction of increasing access to goods and services for the bureaucracy itself.' Above all it led, despite Mandel's claim to the contrary, to a massive rate of accumulation. And this accumulation was not of the 'goods and services' consumed by the bureaucrats, but, above all, of heavy industry – of iron, steel, cement, electricity generation, coal, oil.

The Russian economist, Vasily Selyunin, has recently provided figures on accumulation in the USSR since the late 1920s. He begins with figures from Agabegyan showing 25 per cent of present national income going to 'saving' and 75 per cent to consumption. He then recomputes them to take account of price distortion and concludes, 'the consumption fund accounts for 60 per cent of income and the savings fund for 40 per cent. Such a high composition of savings is, essentially, a wartime standard.'[83] It compares with an average level of gross accumulation in Western states of 15–20 per cent.

Selyunin goes on to show how the real level of accumulation in the USSR has grown continually since the 1920s, giving the following figures: in 1928 consumer goods were 60.5 per cent of output, in 1940 39 per cent, in 1960 27.5 per cent, in 1985 25.2 per cent. He concludes that the officially given figures for the rate of accumulation must be a gross underestimate:

Is it really conceivable that, according to official figures three quarters of net income goes to consumption while consumer goods are only one quarter of industrial output? You can't help wondering what goods are being bought with the consumption fund.

Shifts towards the manufacture of producer goods have put us in the paradoxical situation where accelerated rates of development and more rapid growth in national income have very little effect on the standard of living. The economy is working more and more for itself, rather than for man.[84]

This might be irrational from the point of view of the mass of Russian workers, whose labour is accumulated without them gaining. But it is certainly not a policy based on producing goods for the consumption of the bureaucracy alone – unless you believe that 'steel hard cadres' actually eat the stuff!

The bureaucracy has, in fact, overseen a policy of massive accumulation and industrialisation, and it is completely wrong to claim that it has prevented this occurring.

Secondly, Mandel claims that growth in the 'capital coefficient' is a product of 'the growing non-utilisation of resources, resulting from the general malfunctioning of the economy, as well as by the low productivity of human labour.'

But this is to beg the question. If the non-utilisation of resources is 'growing', why? There is 'general malfunctioning of the economy' and 'low productivity of labour.' But is there any reason for these things to be worse today than in Stalin and Khrushchev's time?

One might expect a Marxist to look more closely at a growth in the 'capital coefficient' than Mandel does. For the coefficient is closely related to the Marxist concept of the organic composition of capital. The coefficient is the ratio of means of production to output, the organic composition the ratio of means of production to labour power (all measured in value terms). If one increases, then the other is likely to do so.

The rising organic composition of capital was, of course, for Marx the basis of the fundamental contradiction of the capitalist economy, the tendency of the rate of profit to decline and of the economy increasingly to stagnate. If it also underlies the crisis of the USSR, then the finding is very significant indeed, and not to be explained away simply by a claim that inefficiency and irrationality are greater now than at the height of Stalin's terror in the 1930s.

Finally, what of the attempt to see the 'fundamental contradiction' as between 'the plan' and 'the market', or between 'bureaucratic despotism' and the 'law of value'?

Mandel's formulation here is both theoretically flawed and politically dangerous.

The law of value operates in societies where there is commodity production – and, in particular, the most developed form of commodity production, capitalist production. The function, necessary to any society, of allocating labour between different productive tasks, is not carried out consciously in such societies, but rather through the blind interaction of the products of different acts of labour which are organized independently of each other. The organizers of these different acts of labour are in competition with each other, and this competition forces them to try to keep ahead of each other in forcing up the productivity of the labour – both through imposing harder work and investing in ever more advanced means of production. By behaving in this way, they are continually relating each act of concrete labour to every other act of concrete labour carried out in the system, or, as Marx put it, transforming concrete individual labour into abstract social labour.

The law of value is the pressure that exists in such a system forcing each individual unit of the system to relate to productivity in every other unit. It is the coercive economic force which overrides the desires and intentions of those who run individual parts of the system. Under capitalism, it is certainly not something which is necessarily opposed to 'bureaucratic despotism' or, for that matter, to planning within individual firms. Quite the opposite – it compels managers to be despotic, to tighten the screw on workers. It also compels them to 'plan' the internal arrangements inside the firm so as to meet the requirement of competition outside it. As Marx put it, 'the anarchy of the market determines the tyranny of the factory.'

What is true is that capitalism is a continually developing system, with innovations and technical progress taking place in some parts of the system before others. Elsewhere in the system the old forms of 'tyranny inside the firm' – the old methods of capitalist planning – then no longer correspond with what is needed to keep abreast in the struggle for increased productivity. The law of value then comes into contradiction with the existing forms of organization of production.

The contradiction between 'bureaucratic despotism' and the 'law of value' occurs because society is subject to the law of value. Can this be true in the USSR? Only if you accept that the USSR is a commodity producing society, a variant of capitalism.

This was no problem for Trotsky and Preobrazhensky writing in the mid-1920s. Although the state controlled big industry in the USSR, virtually the whole of the agricultural sector, a sizeable portion of trade and much handicraft production were in private hands. The state traded with the private sector and with capitalist countries abroad, and therefore was subject to the pressures of commodity production itself. In this situation Trotsky and Preobrazhensky could write about conflicts between the pressures on the one hand from the requirements of commodity production ('the law of value') and on the other from the attempts of the state to plan the economy in the interests of one or other social group.

But where do the pressures to satisfy the requirements of commodity production come from today? Stalin virtually eliminated the rural and urban petty bourgeoisie. The state sector completely dominates the economy. If, as Mandel argues, the USSR is a 'post capitalist society', one no longer dominated by commodity production, then it is difficult to see why the law of value should conflict with the bureaucracy's ways of running the economy. It is rather like expecting the laws of aerodynamics to operate in empty space – unless he is inadvertently admitting what he denies throughout the rest of his book, that the bureaucracy is forced to behave like a capitalist class.

There is one dangerous interpretation which can be put on his formulation: that the bureaucratically administered economy 'contradicts the law of value' through being innately less efficient than a market-based capitalist economy. This, of course, is the contention of a whole host of ideologists of Western capitalism. It is also the contention of many of those who consider the USSR to be a new form of class society, neither capitalist nor socialist: they see it as an 'oriental despotism' or a 'bureaucratic collectivism' with a completely different dynamic to capitalism – indeed, usually with no dynamic at all, and therefore to be regarded as inferior to capitalism. This today, for instance, is essentially the attitude of the group of intellectuals around the magazine *Critique* in Britain. It was also the analysis which led the former American Trotskyist Max Shachtman to support the Bay of Pigs invasion of Cuba. Mandel is not, of course, moving to such horrendous practical conclusions. But he does resort to formulations which might lead others to them, as when he argues, 'clarity and unimpeded dissemination of information ... is guaranteed within capitalist enterprises by private property.'[85]

In fact, precisely because the anarchy of the market does lead to the tyranny of the factory, it also leads to bureaucratic inefficiency within the firm, attempts to stifle innovation, a lack of control of top management over shopfloor management. The functioning of any capitalist firm is characterized by a whole range of practices which are not wiped out by some smooth-running automatic mechanism, but only periodic readjustment of internal production to the external law of value through crisis and 'restructuring.' What is more, the increasing concentration and centralization of capital means that firms get ever larger, the bureaucratic despotism within the firm ever stronger, and the degree of restructuring and crisis required to satisfy the law of value ever greater and more traumatic.

The point is important. All the time we are faced with propaganda from the media telling us that the 'crisis of communism' shows the efficiency of Western capitalism. We should not give an inch on this argument.

Unfortunately, this is not the only point at which Mandel gives ground. At another point he says the reason the USSR's health service is worse than that of the US is that 'doctors in the USSR spend a lot of their time form filling.'[86] Yet American health provision is notoriously inefficient (consuming three times the proportion of the national product compared with the USSR's, or six times the total funds) precisely because American doctors spend a lot of time checking the bank balances of their patients!

The lack of theoretical coherence in Mandel's analysis is revealed most starkly when he writes that the approach of 'Stephen Cohen and Moshe Lewin' is 'similar to that of the present author.'[87] Both Cohen and Lewin have produced useful historical works. But both are also unreconstructed Bukharinites, who believe that reliance on the market would have solved all the USSR's economic problems in the 1930s and who see their task as to advise the USSR's leaders to follow a policy of such reliance today.

A final, practical point on Mandel's analysis. Trotsky viewed the bureaucracy as an unstable, parasitic growth. This led him to conclude that the great crisis he expected in 'a few years, if not a few months' would result in the main sections of the bureaucracy opting to transform themselves into a bourgeois class based on private property, 'not organically through degeneration, but through counter-revolution.'[88]

Those who base themselves on the letter of Trotsky's analysis today are split into three camps. There are those who see the present crisis in the USSR as the one he warned of (ignoring the 55-year time lag, during which the bureaucracy has presided over a massive advance in the forces of production). They draw the conclusion that the reformers inside the USSR and Eastern Europe who talk today about the market represent the forces of 'bourgeois restorationism' and that the task of revolutionaries is to oppose them. The logic of that position is to give critical support to the Ligachevites – the most reactionary forces in the USSR.

The second interpretation is to say that Gorbachev's reforms constitute the 'political revolution', and to offer him critical support.

The third view, the one which Mandel mostly holds to in his book (although, as we have seen, not consistently), is to seek to exploit the openings provided by *Glasnost* to organize the working class independently of Gorbachev and his conservative opponents.

But Mandel can only do so by downplaying those of Trotsky's arguments which insist on the strength of the 'restorationist' forces. Mandel insists, 'It is not capitalism that Gorbachev wants to introduce in the Soviet Union'[89] – although with typical inconsistency he writes elsewhere that 'there has emerged within the bureaucracy a fraction which is clearly restorationist'[90] and that 'Gorbachev's real economic dilemma ... is ... the maintenance of a socialised and planned economy or the restoration of capitalism in large scale industry.'

The fact that such completely different perspectives can emerge from the same 'orthodox Trotskyist' analysis of the USSR must raise questions about the correctness of the analysis itself – just as the crisis of the Trotskyist movement did back in 1947–8.

Cliff reacted to that crisis very differently from Mandel. He argued, in the first, cyclostyled, edition of his book, which appeared early in 1948, that the revolutionary movement faced an enormous danger. Standing by the *letter* of an old analysis of reality could lead to abandoning the revolutionary spirit which originally motivated that analysis. The only way to avoid the danger was to carry through a fundamental re-analysis of Russian society 'rooted in the teachings of the great Marxist teachers.'

Cliff's own analysis began by examining the material realities of the USSR. Sifting through vast masses of empirical material, he drew out the contrasts between conditions in the post-revolutionary period and those after 1928, when Stalin finally consolidated his power.

Trotsky had come to the conclusion in 1935 that Thermidor, the decisive bureaucratization of the regime, had occurred ten years earlier with the defeat of the left opposition. But he had then gone on to point out that Thermidor represented, in the French Revolution, the establishment of a non-revolutionary regime which still preserved essential advances of the revolution, and was different from counter-revolution.

Cliff argued that an examination of material realities showed that further qualitative change had taken place after the Russian Thermidor of 1924. In the winter of 1928–9 the bureaucracy, which had previously balanced between the working class and the peasantry, hit out viciously against both.

The last elements of workers' control were destroyed in the factories; trade union independence was completely abolished; real wages fell 30 or 40 per cent; the GPU was given a free hand to obliterate the last remnants of discussion inside the party; the fight against 'egalitarianism' became state policy as differentials between bureaucrats and workers increased massively; the peasants were driven from the land through so-called 'collectivisation'; the number of prisoners in labour camps rose 20 fold in two years (rising tenfold again in the next decade); Russification was used to destroy the autonomy of the non-Russian Soviet republics.

The fact that all these changes occurred at once was no accident. They were all by-products of the response of the Stalinist wing of the bureaucracy to the economic crisis which hit the country with the threat of war in 1927 and the 'scissors crises of 1928.' As its old policy – the Bukharin-Stalin policy of 1924–7, of ignoring the rest of the world and hoping for the best – fell apart, the bureaucracy used all the forces at its disposal to impose a new policy. It sought to respond to threats from the West by copying the very means used by Western capitalists to build up industry and, with it, military potential. It destroyed the independence of the working class and the peasantry and attacked their living standards so as to gain a surplus for industrialisation. If its methods were even more vicious than those used in the industrial revolution in, say, England it was because the Stalinist bureaucracy sought to do in a couple of decades what had taken 300 years to accomplish in England.

The most impressive part of Cliff's book was where he showed, by meticulous examination of the USSR's official statistics, how the official talk of 'planning' (accepted at the time by Mandel and other 'orthodox Trotskyists') concealed the reality of the continual subordination after 1928 of the production of consumer goods to means of production. While before 1928 consumer and producer goods production both rose together, after 1928 their paths diverged completely. While 'plan' targets for producers' goods were over-fulfilled, those for consumer goods were simply ignored.

This, incidentally, shows the sharp contrast between the notion of planning and industrial development which Trotsky had fought for in the years before 1928 and that which Stalin had implemented. Trotsky had based himself on the need to speed up the rate of industrial growth so as to improve the living standards, the confidence and the social weight of the working class. Stalin based himself on cutting living standards, using the GPU to terrorise the working class into submission, and swamping old, class conscious layers of workers in a sea of raw, inexperienced and terrified ex-peasants.

There were formal similarities between Stalin's policies and Trotsky's. These confused Trotsky himself for a time and led people like Radek and Preobrazhensky to capitulate to Stalinism. But, as Trotsky himself came to realise, from a working-class standpoint they were opposites.

Under Stalin the overall picture was of an economy in which the drive to accumulate means of production dominated everything else. This drive to accumulate pitted the bureaucracy against the workers and peasants. It gave the different members of the bureaucracy interests, rooted in the production process itself, which forged them into a class in unrelenting historical opposition to other classes. It meant they were no longer a stratum of the working class, or a group simply balancing between other classes, but the protagonists of developing a mode of production at the expense of other classes. As Cliff put it:

Why was the first five-year plan such a turning point?
It was now, for the first time, that the bureaucracy sought to create a proletariat and to accumulate capital rapidly. In other words, it was now that the bureaucracy

*sought to accomplish the historical mission of the bour-
geoisie as quickly as possible. A quick accumulation of
capital on the basis of a low level of production, of a small
national income per capita, must put a burdensome pressure on the consumption of the masses, on their living
standards. Under such circumstances the bureaucracy,
transformed into a personification of capital, for whom
the accumulation of capital is the be-all and end-all, must
get rid of all remnants of workers' control, must substitute conviction in the labour process by coercion, must
atomise the working class, must force all socio-political
life into a totalitarian mould. It is obvious that the bureaucracy, which became necessary in the process of capital
accumulation, and which became the oppressor of the
workers, would not be tardy in making use of its social
supremacy in the relations of production in order to gain
advantages for itself in the relations of distribution. Thus
industrialisation and technical revolution in agriculture
('collectivisation') in a backward country under conditions
of siege transforms the bureaucracy from a layer which
is under the direct and indirect pressure and control of
the proletariat into a ruling class, into a manager of the
'general business of society: the direction of labour, affairs
of state, justice, science, art and so forth.'* [91]

Cliff refers to the bureaucracy as 'state capitalist.' This has
caused his theory to be attacked by a host of commentators
– of which Mandel is just one – who claim there cannot be
capitalism without private owners of the means of production
competing with each other to sell goods.

Cliff deals with this argument at length in his book. He
bases himself on the analyses of the imperialist stage of capitalism developed during the First World War by Lenin and by
the young Bukharin. These showed how the concentration
and centralization of capital leads to the replacement of 'free
market' capitalism by 'state monopoly capitalism.' Horizontal
and vertical mergers lead to huge firms which dominate
whole industries, planning their operations with meticulous

care and not just leaving them to the accidents of the market. The heads of these industries work increasingly closely with the state bureaucracies. There is, so to speak, a 'merging together' of industry and the state. This merging finds its fullest development in all-out imperialist wars, in which the state and capital work together to plan the war economy internally, while seeking to destroy rival capitalisms physically.

So much is the war economy planned, that those who base themselves on a simple, ahistorical view of capitalism do not see it any longer as capitalist. This was, for instance, the conclusion which the famous Austro-Marxist economist, Hilferding, came to about the Nazi German economy. For *inside* the war economy production is planned from above and does not depend upon the ups and downs of the market, upon the interplay of commodities. And its external trade is necessarily limited.

Cliff insists, however, that the war economy remains a species of capitalism. For if old-style 'free market' competition plays a very little role, a new form of competition dominates it completely. This is military competition between the rival state capitalist ruling classes of different countries. This competition has similar effects on the organization of production inside each country to those economic competition has on the organization of production inside each firm.

To compete militarily with each other the rulers of each country have to make sure that the productivity of the labour under their command does not fall below that of their rivals. Every time their rivals invest in new equipment and more advanced technology they have to try to do the same. Every time their rivals succeed in getting a bigger surplus for investment by increasing the rate of exploitation of their workers, they have to try to match their efforts.

In this way, the different acts of concrete labour carried out in different factories in different parts of the world are related to each other, are measured against each other, are transmuted into expressions of a common abstract labour. The threat of military defeat compels the giant state capitalist ruling class to impose the law of value on its enterprises just as the smallest individual entrepreneur is forced to by the threat of bankruptcy.

It is this analysis which Cliff uses to decipher the puzzle of Stalinist Russia. Stalin's policies after 1928 involved transforming Russia into a massive arms economy, dominated by the drive to accumulate the economic basis of military power, above all heavy industry. Stalin was subordinating the USSR's economy as a whole to the pressures of a particular form of international capitalist competition (to the law of value on a world scale), even while preventing competition between different sections of the economy inside the USSR.

It is this domination by competition which explains the most remarkable feature of the USSR's economic development: the way in which it has displayed the very dynamic which Marx argued was unique to capitalism – the endless pursuit of accumulation. In the *Communist Manifesto* Marx makes a sharp distinction between 'bourgeois society' in which 'living labour is but a means to increase accumulated labour' and 'communist society' where 'accumulated labour is but a means to widen, to enrich, to promote the existence of the labourer.' The USSR lies on the side of 'bourgeois society' in this respect and not on the side of socialism. Cliff shows why.

But that is not all he seeks to do. His aim in exposing the dynamic of the USSR's economy as one of endless competitive accumulation is to draw conclusions for the struggle for socialism.

Those who do not identify such a dynamic can come to one of two equally disastrous conclusions. The first is to see the bureaucratic ruling stratum as more progressive than the capitalist classes of the West. The logic is then to subordinate the struggle for socialism to giving assistance, or at least advice, to these rulers. It is a logic that leads to horror at the thought that social upheavals might threaten their rule, and to paralysis in the face of the present crisis in the USSR through fear of it leading to a 'restoration of capitalism.'

The second conclusion is to see the bureaucracy as less progressive than Western capitalist classes, as a totalitarian force preventing human development for the indefinite future. Such was the path of Shachtman in the 1940s and 1950s. Such is the path that many 'new class theorists' are tempted towards today.

Cliff's theory, by identifying such a dynamic, comes to a radically distinct conclusion. It is that the Stalinist bureaucracy, like the Western capitalist classes, creates its own gravedigger. The more successful it is in accumulating capital, the more it builds up the size and strength of a working class that has the potential to overthrow it.

The bureaucracy increases the working class on the basis of the highest concentration history has yet known. And, try as it might to abridge the abyss between concentrated wage labour and concentrated capital, the bureaucracy is bringing into being a force that will sooner or later clash violently with it.[92]

When these words were written in the late 1940s, they seemed much less impressive than those who talked of 'hundreds of years of degenerated workers' states' or those who claimed the Russian bureaucracy ruled over some new variant of slave society which was not subject to the contradictions of capitalism. They are vindicated today by the scale of unrest which is sweeping the USSR.

One last point. Only Cliff's analysis enables us to account for the character of the present economic crisis in the USSR. It is because the USSR is part of a world system based on military and economic competition that the bureaucracy finds its old methods of running the economy no longer fit.

The USSR's rulers try to maintain military parity with a state which has twice their GNP – and so have to spend twice the proportion of their own GNP on arms. They are obsessed with modernising their engineering industries so that they match technical advance elsewhere in the world. They see the relative fall in the price of their major export, oil, in recent years as a threat to their whole economic strategy by making it more difficult to import the most advanced machines. Above all, they are deeply afraid that they cannot raise the productivity of labour inside the USSR closer to the US level.

Mandel used to deny that external circumstances could exercise such pressures on the Russian economy, writing that this was to claim 'that the tail of one per cent of output imported from and exported to advanced capitalist countries is wagging the dog of the Russian economy.'[93] Now he admits they exist, but cannot integrate them into a total analysis. And so, as we have seen, he sees a contradiction between 'the law of value' and 'bureaucratic despotism' without explaining how that law operates and why the contradiction should come to the fore now.

Yet once you recognize the USSR as a bureaucratic state capitalist country, it is very easy to complete the analysis. The Stalinist bureaucracy responded to the world crisis of the 1930s and the growing threat of war by seeking to accumulate capital inside the country while cutting to a minimum its external trade links. In this respect, it was not behaving very differently from ruling classes in many Western and Third World capitalist countries. The whole period was one of relatively self-contained economies in which the state intervened in order to prevent the onset of violent crises within the internal economy – the period of Keynesianism in the West, of import substitutionist growth in countries like Argentina and Brazil, and of attempts to copy Stalinist 'planning' in China and even India.

But in the 1960s and 1970s such approaches everywhere ran increasingly into contradiction with the internationalization of the world economy. The concentration of capital meant that the resources required to keep ahead in the most advanced industries began to exceed the internal resources of nearly all states; keeping up with advances in technology increasingly meant forging links with the largest multinational corporations. The industries which had developed within the confines of national boundaries could now only survive if they were restructured as part of a new international division of labour.

The restructuring could be painful even for relatively open and limited state capitalisms like that of Britain. In the more autarchic and complete state capitalisms of the East it can be devastating. It threatens not only the conditions and livelihoods of many workers, but whole sections of the bureaucratic-managerial apparatus itself. And there can be no guarantee that even if it is successfully completed conditions in the outside world won't have shifted in the interim, leaving the USSR's economy still uncompetitive.

The Russian ruling class faces the problem that periodically besets every capitalist ruling class. The very methods that allowed successful accumulation in the past no longer do so. Because it is part of a world system it has to try to change its ways. But its attempts to do so are unleashing social forces which it cannot control. As Marx wrote in the *Communist Manifesto*:

> *The bourgeoisie cannot exist without constantly revolutionising the instruments of production, and thereby the relations of productions and with them the whole relations of society ... Constant revolutionising of production, uninterrupted disturbances of all social conditions, everlasting uncertainty and agitation distinguishes the bourgeois epoch from all earlier ones. All fixed fast frozen relationships, with their train of ancient and venerable prejudices and opinions are swept away, all newly formed ones become antiquated before they can ossify. All that is solid melts into air, all that is holy is profaned, and man is at last compelled to face with sober senses his conditions of life and his relations with his kind.*[94]

The Stalinist state bourgeoisies of the East can no more escape from this violent, capitalist dynamic than can the 'private' (more accurately, the state monopoly capitalist) bourgeoisies of the West and Third World. That is what is so exciting about what is happening in the USSR today. But to understand why, you have to move beyond the vague, inconsistent, self-contradictory formulations of Mandel, and the best way to do so is to base yourself on Cliff's book.

A theory which has not withstood the test of facts

Ernest Mandel

Tony Cliff based his theory that the USSR and countries with analogous socio-economic structures are 'state-capitalist' on a set of hypotheses which are taken as axiomatic. We shall outline six of them:
1. Soviet society and the societies of Western Europe, of the United States and of Japan are all qualitatively the same since they are all capitalist.

2. In the USSR a new ruling class exists which is not based on private property but which can nevertheless be characterized as capitalist.

3. The Soviet economy is fundamentally ruled by the law of value, 'operating via the world market', even though internal competition has been eliminated.

4. Just like Western and Japanese capitalists, the Russian ruling class is basically driven by the need to accumulate: 'production for the sake of production.'

5. Crises of overproduction are absent because 'organized capitalism' allows them to be avoided in the USSR.[95]

6. Furthermore, general crises of overproduction do not exist in the imperialist countries either, in view of the tendency towards 'organized capitalism' and the importance of the armaments sector in their economies.

Events over the last 15 years have inflicted one cruel blow after the other on these dogmatic assertions.[96] The generalized recessions of the world capitalist economy in 1974–75 and 1980–82 were truly classic crises of overproduction, the mitigating effects of inflation notwithstanding. In scale they exceeded, rather than being below, the average capitalist crisis of overproduction of the last century and a half. What then remains of the myth of 'organized capitalism' and Hilferding's *Generalkartell*?

Nothing similar has taken place in the USSR. If there is a crisis in that country it is one of underproduction of use values (of scarcity) and not one of overproduction of exchange values (of commodities). To claim that the first is only a variant of the second is a gross fallacy. An empty shop is not 'a variant' of a shop stuffed full of unsellable goods.

A process of restoration of capitalism is under way in several East European countries.[97] In at least one country, the GDR, that process is almost complete. Literally no one in these countries, or in the world, denies the evidence. This presents the followers of the theory of state capitalism with an insoluble problem: how is it possible under capitalism to restore capitalism?

They try to get out of this difficulty by claiming that 'private capitalism' is different from 'state capitalism.' But that only pushes the problem one stage further back: either the difference between 'state' and 'private' capitalism is a qualitative one – in which case, why use the same concept to cover both? Or the difference is purely quantitative. In which case, the whole initial problem re-emerges more strongly. Can one seriously argue that there was only a quantitative difference between the GDR and the Federal Republic? Does the Federal Republic's *Anschluss* change nothing basic in the GDR's actual socio-economic system? Are the societies of North and South Korea qualitatively the same?

To reduce the nature of capitalism simply to the wish to accumulate ('production for the sake of production') is to dismiss much of Volumes 1 and 3 of *Capital*, and the whole of Volume 2. Capitalist production is generalized commodity production. Every commodity contains within itself a contradiction between use value and exchange value, as well as a contradiction between commodity and money. An 'organized capitalism' that overcame these contradictions would no longer be capitalism, at least not in the sense analysed and defined by Marx.

Capital exists and can only exist with money-capital as its starting point. Capital is value looking to increase in value, to surplus value. Of necessity it must eventually recover its initial money form, despite the fact that while engaged in the production process it no longer has that form. Without money there can be no capital accumulation.

These are not esoteric abstractions. We are at the heart of the matter. It is of no use for a capitalist just to make the workers he exploits produce the maximum of surplus value. He cannot transform a car pound or warehouses full of colour televisions into additional machines or steel, or into wages for extra workers, or into private jets for his own consumption. He cannot accumulate capital simply by producing surplus value. He must realise that surplus value through the sale of the commodities that have been produced in order to accumulate capital. As Marx says, the process of (expanded) reproduction, that is to say, the process of accumulation, is the unity of both the process of production and the process of realisation of surplus value. These two never coincide automatically. Without the process of realisation no accumulation is possible. What makes periodic crises of overproduction inevitable is the inevitable contradiction between the two poles of this unity. Moreover, the same contradiction activates a series of mechanisms typical of the capitalist economy. These were carefully analysed by Marx and can be called 'the laws of motion' of the capitalist economy.

To know whether a society is basically capitalist or not we have therefore to ask the question (and back it up factually): are the laws of capitalist motion in evidence?

Just to point to the extraction of surplus labour from the direct producers is insufficient. At night all cats are grey. For thousands of years since primitive communism surplus labour has always been extracted from the direct producers, and this will continue until we reach the future classless socialist society. But that does not make all these societies capitalist. Marx says that in the last analysis the nature of each society (except classless society) is determined by the specific form in which surplus labour is extracted (*Marx Engels Werke*, Vol. 27, p. 799). And under capitalism that takes the specific form of the transformation of labour power into a commodity, of its sale to capitalists for money, of capitalists buying the means of production for money, of the appropriation by these same capitalists of the products of wage labour, and of the sale of these commodities in order to make roughly the average profit. Without all these specific mechanisms, capitalism does not exist for Marx, at least not as a dominant mode of production.

Our interpretation of the present-day capitalist economy and of present-day Soviet economy allows the inner coherence of Marxist theory to be preserved. Cliff's theory destroys any type of coherence unless essential elements of Marxist theory are jettisoned. So whatever advantage it claims in explaining the USSR is lost when it comes to explaining present day capitalism.

The idea of the bureaucracy as a ruling class really has to be taken with a smile after what has happened in Hungary, Poland and the GDR (to quote only those examples). Has any ruling class in history ever been seen to literally tiptoe away from the stage of society, as a significant section of the *nomenklatura* in those countries is now doing?

According to chapter one of Volume 1 of *Capital*, a commodity is only a commodity because it is the product of private acts of labour performed independently one from the other. To present the Soviet economy in terms of a capitalist economy therefore implies that industrial labour there consists of 'private acts of labour performed independently one from the other': an absurd description if ever there was one.

To say that an act of labour is private means that no capitalist (firm) knows whether the labour costs expended (both living and dead) will be recognized as socially necessary costs, that is to say, whether they will be paid for by society. It is only after the sale of the commodities that the capitalist learns whether he has gained or lost. If the labour expended has been socially necessary, he obtains an average profit. If social labour has been wasted, he gets less than the average profit or goes bankrupt.

At the first sign of sale at a loss or of below average profits, he attempts to change the way in which production is organized. He will try to improve the technology, to use better machines, to save on raw materials and energy, to extract more surplus labour from his workforce, to spread his investments, to get access to cheaper credit, and so on. The organization of labour depends in the first place on the private decisions of the factory owner, which is then corrected by competition, by the market. He has to submit to these corrections or face extinction. Under capitalism there is only one overall measure of performance – realised profit. The more productivity is raised, and the lower the costs of production, the greater the likelihood that his profit will outstrip that of his competitors. But there is nothing automatic about this. It is the post-sale profits that determine everything. The capitalist economy is an economy based on profit, and profit can only be realised and measured in the form of money.

This is where the famous 'law of value' enters into play. It determines the social nature of labour through commodities exchanging at equivalent values and so operates under capitalism as the tendency to create an average rate of profit. Capitals move out of enterprises and sectors of below average profit into those of above average profit. Thus, as Harman himself emphasizes, the essential function of the law of value under capitalism is to ensure that productive resources are allocated through objective mechanisms, these being imposed on enterprises and capitalists, as well as on workers, behind their backs and independently of their will and decisions.

However, the law of value only rules any economy in so far as it is one of generalized commodity production, that is, one in which labour is basically private labour. In pre-capitalist societies this is not the case. Here the law of value is not determinant, even if it has already begun to influence economic decisions. A French peasant of the 11th century, a Russian peasant of the 18th century, or a Peruvian peasant of the first half of the 20th century, does not alter his decisions to sow or reap in line with the price of wheat rising or falling, for the simple reason that 95 per cent of his production is not for the market. In these societies the bulk of productive resources are directly allocated to different sectors by those who control the means of production. Direct, *a priori* allocation is the opposite of *a posteriori* allocation brought about through the law of value. This difference between two methods of resource allocation marks the opposition between planning and the market.

In the USSR the essential investments are not decided via the law of value. They are decided by the bureaucracy, mostly at state level. It is a planned economy (that implies no value judgement: an economy can be planned in an irrational, even senseless manner) as far as direct allocation of resources is concerned. For 70 years, 'loss' making enterprises requiring large subsidies have received a preferential allocation of productive resources. These have been systematically diverted from 'more profitable' enterprises or sectors. Such phenomena are unthinkable under capitalism and the rule of the law of value. But if the law of value does not rule 'directly' in the USSR, does it do so 'indirectly' through the intermediary of the world market?

Dogmatically, as if it were a revealed truth, Cliff and Harman claim this to be the case. They cannot prove it. Any rule of the law of value 'through the intermediary of the world market' has to operate via trade, like anything to do with capitalism. Enterprises that fail to compete with imported goods are doomed to go under. At least two thirds, if not more, of Soviet enterprises do not compete with imperialist enterprises. If they were subject to the law of value operating 'through the intermediary of the world market', they would be forced to close (like Mexican steelworks or British coal mines). There is therefore no 'rule of the law of value' in the USSR 'through the intermediary of the world market.'

A hybrid economy

However, even though the functioning of the Soviet economy is not dominated by the law of value, it cannot abstract itself from its influence. While it is not a capitalist economy, that is, an economy based on generalized commodity production, neither is it a socialist economy geared to the direct satisfaction of human need, an economy in which labour possesses an immediately social character. It is a post-capitalist economy with elements of the market. Partial survival of commodity production is combined with the partial rule of the direct allocation of productive resources.

This combination is hybrid and contradictory. It implies that the fate of the USSR as a transitional society between capitalism and socialism, 'frozen' at its present stage by the bureaucratic dictatorship, has not yet been settled historically. A social counter-revolution can pull the USSR back towards capitalism. A victorious anti-bureaucratic political revolution can push it in the direction of socialism (no more than that: socialism in one country is impossible no matter how pure, democratic, revolutionary or internationalist a government based on workers' power may be).

Comrades from the Socialist Workers Party in Britain (SWP) find this notion of hybrid combination, the perpetuation of which lacks all certainty, this 'transition between two progressive modes of production' (to quote Marx's celebrated formula), difficult to accept and understand. They are quite wrong. We are talking here of a phenomenon that has occurred in practically every epoch when a given mode of production has entered its historical period of decline and decay.

To give just one example – between the decline of the feudal mode of production and the triumph of capitalism a transitional epoch intervened in which petty commodity production dominated, stretching over several centuries. Petty commodity production has its own characteristics which are neither those of feudalism (serfdom) or of capitalism (wage labour). The predominant form of labour is the free labour of small proprietors or semi-proprietors, owning their own means of production.

We are not talking here of a new mode of production able to perpetuate itself automatically. Petty commodity production is capable of regression towards feudalism, which is what happened in a large area of central and eastern Europe from the 16th century onwards, the period of the 'second serfdom.' It is also capable of moving towards capitalism, that is towards the predominance of wage labour, which is what happened in the Netherlands and in England from the 17th and 18th centuries onwards. But in both cases the small independent producers disappeared only little by little.

The same rule can be applied more or less to the period of transition between capitalism and socialism. Either what remains of commodity production will finally eliminate most of the direct appropriation and allocation of the social surplus product – in which case, capitalism will be restored. Or society will throw off the deadweight of the bureaucracy and ensure that the direct appropriation and allocation of major resources for the satisfaction of needs as democratically decided by the masses will predominate – in which case, the unavoidable survival of some market mechanisms will no longer be able to put a brake on genuine progress towards socialism. But in both cases, what is specific about today's hybrid Soviet situation will have largely disappeared.

Once again, it is not a question of some abstract theoretical schema. Our understanding of the principal causes of the specific economic crisis characteristic of the USSR is rooted in reality. Current mystification notwithstanding, what the Soviet economy suffers from is at one and the same time too little central planning (democratic planning, let it be understood, not bureaucratic planning) and too little of the market (in all those areas where as a result of the inadequate objective socialisation of labour direct allocation of resources does not operate and the market is required to break up monopolies).[98]

The despotic nature of planning from the First Five Year Plan onwards meant that it was marked by colossal disproportions, the cumulative effect of which in the end undermined even the very targets set by the bureaucracy. The market or pseudo-market mechanisms used have always lacked a proper foundation largely because there is no unified pricing system and no stable currency. The double pricing system is an accurate reflection of the hybrid dualism of the Soviet economy.[99]

Comrade Cliff's analysis makes much of the importance of the world market for the Soviet economy. But the world market is not some disembodied Holy Ghost hovering above the clouds in order to create the world, as the Bible boldly tells us. One of the essential contributions that Marx and Marxism have brought to the social sciences is the categorical rejection of any kind of reification of economic categories. One of the essential gains of historical materialism is to discover behind these categories relations between social groups (social classes and major class fractions). The connections between them and the way they struggle for their interests strips bare the secret of economic categories, including that of the world market.

In this respect, the theory put forward by Trotsky and the Fourth International, that the fate of the USSR and so of its economy has not yet been definitely settled, is based on a precise understanding of international class struggle in the 20th century. Cliff's theory largely empties the interconnection between international class struggle and what has happened in the USSR of its significance.

Trotsky predicted in 1905–6 that the imperialist chain would first break in Russia because its proletariat was subjectively stronger than the proletariat in Germany and other countries. Objectively, however, the conditions for an advance towards socialism were infinitely worse in Russia than in any of the major industrialised countries in the world. Therefore either the victorious Russian revolution would join up with a victorious revolution in some of these countries, in which case the proletariat would retain political power. Or it would not, in which case the Russian proletariat would lose political power.

But what would be the precise form of the counter-revolution in Russia? Again, that did not depend first and foremost on the forces present in that country alone, but on the relationship of social and political forces at a world level. The imperialist bourgeoisie was strong enough to prevent (or, what amounts to the same thing, the leadership of the proletariat was too weak to ensure) the victory of the revolution in Germany, Austria, Italy, Britain, France and Spain. It was not, however, in a position to crush the world working class movement. Overall, it was only strong enough to crush the workers' movement in Germany and Spain with the victory of fascism, but even that was only temporary.

Furthermore, the Russian bourgeoisie had been too weakened, and the international bourgeoisie was too divided, to make a success of restoring capitalism by civil war, foreign intervention or the direct pressure of the world market. In part, this effort was neutralized by the intervention and pressure of the world proletariat.[100] What followed as a result was a relative world equilibrium of class forces. These conditions meant that a political counter-revolution (Thermidor) took place in Russia, but not a social one. The proletariat lost political power but it was not an old or new capitalist class which benefitted but, to use Marx's formula, functionaries who rose from the ranks of the working class itself.

In the long term, this relative equilibrium of class forces cannot last. Either the international working class will make decisive moves forward to socialist revolution in key countries of the world, in which case any restoration of capitalism will become impossible in the USSR. Or the world proletariat will experience crushing defeats, not necessarily in the precise form of the Nazi victory in Germany but with similar consequences, namely the elimination for a long period of its capacity for resistance and collective and organized action. If that happens the restoration of capitalism in the USSR is inevitable. Given this perspective, the role of the Soviet working class itself, its capacity to react, to resist and move onto the counter-offensive, will become more and more important.

Chris Harman criticises us by quoting an extract from an article written in 1956, in which we stated that the Soviet economy grows in a regular rhythm and that this shows its superiority to the capitalist economy. Extracting a single quotation on a topic which an author has written about for more than 40 years is not a serious way to debate. We could quite easily refer to ten or so passages in which we predicted that the rate of growth in the Soviet economy would fall. One quotation will do:

> *The disproportion between the development of light indus-*
> *try and that of heavy industry, which underlies the bureau-*
> *cratic form of management, has become a deep-going*
> *weakness in the economic system. Its repercussions on*
> *the development of heavy industry itself ... are becoming*
> *bigger and bigger.* [101]

So have we changed our mind on this matter? Is there a contradiction in our analysis? Not at all. The quotation and the method used by Harman can be turned against him. If one examines the real growth curve of the Soviet economy from 1928 onwards (excepting the years of Nazi aggression against the USSR 1941–44), it will be seen: a) that growth really was regular and uninterrupted; b) that unlike the capitalist economy the USSR has experienced no recession, no crisis of over-production leading to an absolute fall in production, for more than 60 years;[102] c) that the rate of growth began to fall 20 years ago; d) that this fall may become 'zero growth', but that there is no 'law' making this inevitable. It so happens, then, that we did predict this fall in the rate of growth and our analysis of the Soviet economy (and of Soviet society) accounts perfectly for both aspects of the tendency.

Cliff's explanation, on the other hand, starts from a confusion in analysis and terminology and relies on false statistical data. Under capitalism, the lash of competition and of class struggle leads capitalists to increase the organic composition of capital. In the first instance they replace living by dead labour, i.e. by machines, in order to sell more cheaply on the market. In the second they can raise the rate of surplus value by subjecting workers to the pressure of unemployment. The rise in the organic composition of capital, and the resultant tendency of the rate of profit to fall, are the consequence and not the cause of this behaviour. The cause lies in the nature of the system itself: production for the sake of profit. This takes us back again to money-capital, which is the starting point for the reproduction cycle of capital and its end point.

In other words, without competition between capitalist firms, none of this dynamic would exist, or would only exist on an extremely limited scale.[103] Marx was explicit on the subject. He writes in Volume 3 of *Capital* that without competition 'the fire that keeps production alive' (and *a fortiori* accumulation) would be extinguished. Let us add that Marx believed that capitalism can only exist in the form of 'many capitals', which in turn inevitably implies competition. Marx was also quite unambiguous about the point that competition involves exchange, that competition is only possible through exchange. So where is the 'exchange' between Soviet arms and imperialist goods?

The use of the term 'military competition' as equivalent to competition for the realisation of profit arises from a characteristic semantic confusion. In reality, for 'military competition' to be capitalist competition, it must operate via the world market. That would mean the USSR being forced to buy arms or the machines necessary for the production of arms from abroad, which would mean that Soviet factories producing these arms or machines would have to close if they worked at too high a cost price. This has clearly not been the case in the USSR for 70 years. Quite the contrary. No arms factory or factory making machines for arms has closed, irrespective of whether costs were known to be higher than those in the USA, Germany or Japan.

All this proves once again that the Soviet economy is not governed by the law of value. And so one cannot speak of 'competition' with capitalist countries in the economic Marxist sense of the word when dealing with the arms race.

Do the figures quoted by Harman agree with reality? Not at all. What they reflect is the systematic attempt to camouflage the reality of the Soviet economy which the bureaucracy has carried out since the Stalin era. This has misled both apologists like Maurice Dobb and critics like Bordiga and Cliff. The aim of this mystification is to disguise the essentially parasitic and wasteful role of bureaucratic management.

The theoretical error which allows this statistical falsification is the reduction of the Soviet economy to a system having two instead of three sectors (Department III includes unproductive consumption and 'accumulation', while Department I consists of means of production and Department II of the means of consumption consumed by the producers, that is to say productive consumption). With a two-sector scheme, productive and unproductive consumption, investment which leads to expanded reproduction and investment which serves no economic purpose in reproduction are carelessly added together and jumbled up.

Here is an example, deliberately chosen from outside armaments production. When a steel mill produces bars of steel which 'accumulate' in warehouses (or, better still, in the open air) and remain there, one cannot speak of 'accumulation' in any economic sense of the word. Using the term 'capital accumulation' in this connection would make any real capitalist laugh. It is clearly waste production from a social point of view. It is also waste production from the point of view of those who control the economy.

Sheer wastage of products and resources occupies an enormous space in the Soviet economy. Calculation of its size is not easy, but the most critical economists have put forward the figure of between 30 and 40 per cent of available productive resources (including human resources: a third of all paid hours of work result in no real production). Here we have the 'secret' of the command economy, of pseudo – or semi-planning in the USSR: it is Department III which is over-expanded, not Department I.

Let us take one concrete example among many. The USSR is the biggest producer of chemical fertiliser in the world. It produces nearly as much as the USA and Western Europe put together. Does this imply overexpansion of Department I (chemical fertiliser, being a raw material, is part of Department I)? Not at all. More than half this production is lost 'in transit.' It never reaches the user and so is never incorporated into any force of production or reproduction. A product of labour whose use value is not realised has no exchange value. So asserts Marx for commodity production. To extend this analysis to any society not governed by the law of value, to say it is simply a sheer waste of social resources, is to echo the spirit of his thought still more strongly. Such wastage has nothing to do with any supposed 'allocation of productive resources by the law of value' or with any drive to 'accumulate capital.'

Back will come the retort, but what about armaments production under capitalism? Isn't that also waste production of productive resources? Wouldn't capitalism which incorporates the arms race as a more or less permanent feature be a capitalism which develops the forces of destruction rather than the forces of production?[104] Our answer to this objection is at several levels.

From the point of view of the individual capitalist firm involved in arms production this is not waste. Such commodities find buyers in so far as these buyers (the state or arms dealers) wish to realise their use value. So they possess an exchange value which creates real profit. Otherwise they wouldn't be produced under capitalism anyway.

Isn't what the firm producing arms finds 'useful' irrational, even inhuman, from the social point of view? Undoubtedly. But this is absolutely characteristic of capitalism. The contradiction between the partial rationality and the global irrationality of economic activity is developed to the extreme.[105] The same point can be made about drugs, cigarettes, polluting automobiles, chemical fertilisers, nuclear power stations, and so on.

Is arms production 'unproductive' from the point of view of the capitalist economy as a whole? That is, doesn't it fail to increase the mass of surplus value, of profit-source and of capital, which is the only definition of 'productive' from the point of view of capital as a whole? Not necessarily. When a mass of productive resources lies idle the effect of expanding Department III can be to mobilize these resources and so increase the total mass of surplus value and of profits.[106] That is clearly what happened in the United States from 1940 onwards. It would be absurd to deny that capitalism, and indeed bourgeois American society, was more prosperous in 1944 (not to say in 1950) than in 1933.

Does that mean that capitalism has been transformed into a 'waste economy'? Only partially. Besides there is nothing new about this. Marx already stated in the *Grundrisse* and in *Capital* that capitalism can only develop the production of material wealth by simultaneously undermining the two sources of all wealth: human productive force and nature. During the rise of capitalism the 'positive' effects of growth outweighed the destructive ones. In its period of decline, from 1914 at least, the opposite has been the case. Yet growth since 1949 (in the USA since 1940) has not been any the less real. The extra amount of foodstuff, textiles, medicines, housing and domestic appliances produced in the last 40 years is genuine and colossal. To label this as 'forces of destruction' is absurd, non-materialist and non-Marxist.

Should one conclude from this that it is a matter of indifference, economically speaking, whether society produces means of destruction or means of production? Such a conclusion is not justified either. The iron laws of reproduction continue to operate in a commodity production system of whatever type (including the partial commodity production system of the USSR, as in any country in a period of transition between capitalism and socialism).

One cannot produce wheat with teargas, dresses with tanks, or television sets with rockets. The dimensions of Department III are bound to have repercussions on the dimensions of Departments I and II. The utilisation of any productive resource for the manufacture of armaments entails its removal from production of the means of production and of consumption. Production in Department III therefore cannot be developed beyond a certain point without in the end reducing production in the other two Departments, thereby strangling expanded reproduction and so the accumulation of capital.

What is true of capitalist society is also true of pre-capitalist society. And in as much as armaments production persists (or other forms of wastage appear on a grand scale) it applies to post-capitalist society as well.

For thousands of years in pre-capitalist societies, wars led to famine and to an absolute decline in production which was temporary or long lasting depending on the period and the circumstances. In the USSR the over-expansion in Department III of armaments production and unproductive expenses in general (above all administrative expenses, i.e., the cost of the bureaucracy) puts a brake on the overall development of material production.

In the end it even chokes off growth, including growth in

the arms sector. This is for two reasons: it takes away vital resources for the development of Departments I and II; and it increases the producers' dissatisfaction with their given level of consumption (even if this rises in a modest way), such that their lack of concern about overall production results becomes ever greater. Under capitalism, this lack of concern is partly neutralized by fear of redundancy and unemployment, something which has played no role in the USSR for more than half a century. Instead, therefore, alongside each producer had to be placed a supervisor, a foreman, a cop. Hence the enormously swollen size of the 'petty' bureaucracy, amounting to about 20 million people, it can be reckoned, since Trotsky's time. Hence also the colossal and permanent growth of unproductive expense: Department III is biting its own tail like the legendary serpent.

This mechanism cannot be 'reformed', as Gorbachev has discovered to his cost. The serpent can only be slain by the spread of strictly public, popular working-class control, and by the spread of genuine working-class management in a multi-party socialist democracy.

A schematic system of thought which only operates in black and red and which is the prisoner of outrageously simplistic abstractions is incapable of handling the categories of 'transition', of 'combined and uneven development' and of 'contradictory reality.' In other words, such thought is undialectical. This unfortunately is the way in which Tony Cliff and Chris Harman think, at least when dealing with general problems.

Moreover there is something irrational, even positively irresponsible, in the SWP comrades' vituperative attacks on accelerated industrialisation in the USSR from 1927 onwards. This is clear to the naked eye for every worker, peasant and Marxist from Third World countries, and for every true internationalist.

Each one of us is against 'overinvestment', against 'gigantism', against Stalinist and post-Stalinist 'super industrialisation', most of which represent a total loss of expenditure in material resources. But we are not against accelerated industrialisation as such in these countries or in Russia, which was the first to opt for it, after the October revolution. To turn one's back on this industrialisation would mean not just rejecting the whole short – and medium-term trend in economic policy elaborated by Lenin, Trotsky and the Left Opposition after 1923. Above all it would mean condemning those countries to flounder in barbarism while they wait for the victory of the world revolution. But when would that come about? After five years? After ten years? After 20 years? After 30 years? Who knows? Must we in the meantime fold our arms and tolerate the intolerable?

When we speak of intolerable barbarism we are not speaking loosely. Underdevelopment kills 16 million children in the Third World each year. How many children would die each year if development took place in these countries on the basis of a democratically run socialised economy? The *Generalplan Ost* of Nazi-led German imperialism envisaged the extermination of 100 million people in central and Eastern Europe. Was it wrong not to have laid down conditions for successful resistance against this projected monstrous crime, notably by developing a powerful industry in the Urals and beyond? By rejecting a sense of proportion (the difference between necessary accelerated industrialisation and disproportionate, wasteful and destructive super industrialisation), which breaks with dialectical thinking, the SWP comrades put themselves in an impossible situation with respect to their own objectives.

Let us suppose that one day they succeed in leading the British working class to a seizure of power. What type of society would emerge from this victorious revolution? A socialist society? Have the SWP comrades been suddenly converted to the reactionary Utopia of socialism in one country? A state capitalist society because of 'the pressure of competition from the world market'? Workers' power would scarcely be in a position to counter this pressure in Great Britain alone. Would their efforts then have been in vain? A socialist society by virtue of the fact that the British revolution would immediately spread to the rest of the world? But if that does not happen, or at least not for some time, wouldn't Britain then be a transitional society between capitalism and socialism which all advanced workers and communists/socialists would unite in an effort to protect from the dangers of bureaucratization, even if they couldn't eliminate them entirely? What is the point of rejecting today the very concept which one would be forced to apply tomorrow? And wouldn't the funds for accumulation, productive as well as unproductive, have to be sufficient to meet (at least partially) the requirements to invest in order to satisfy the needs of the masses and to defend them against imperialism?

Wouldn't reducing this whole complex problematic simply to the question of the 'pressure of the world market' result in paralysis, even suicide, for the SWP and for any victorious British revolution? In the imperfect world in which we live it is impossible to find one's bearings or to act in a revolutionary manner without resorting to such categories as 'transition', 'transitional programme', 'transitional demands' and 'transitional society.' The all or nothing approach acts as a blindfold. It also inhibits revolutionary action, no matter how limited in effect.

The specific character of the Soviet bureaucracy

According to Cliff and Harman, the Soviet bureaucracy is characterized by the tendency to excess production of the means of production, the tendency to 'production for the sake of production.' The idea which they object to (and attribute to us) is the claim that the economic development of the USSR is dominated by the production of consumption goods (luxury goods) for the bureaucracy. We have never defended such an extreme thesis. In no society (including slave or feudal society) does what motivates the ruling class or group – the desire to increase its own consumption – explain or exhaust the dynamic of the economy as a whole.

In order to preserve and extend its privileges, the Soviet bureaucracy, just like any ruling class or group in history, has to develop the economy up to a certain point. Without car factories three million middle and top bureaucrats cannot acquire cars. Without enough steel, electricity or iron ore, the car industry cannot be developed satisfactorily. True, one could try and import these goods. But that would mean having to export in order to obtain resources, which would mean submitting to the law of value and to the world market. In that situation an underdeveloped country remains basically an underdeveloped country, unable either to industrialise beyond a certain limit or buy a sufficient number of cars.

In order to avoid just this kind of constraint (to escape the constraints of the world market), the Soviet bureaucracy unleashed a process of 'super industrialisation' in the USSR. Without this, it could not have defended, consolidated or extended its powers and privileges as spectacularly as it did after 1928.

This is the framework necessary to understand the socio-political struggles that have taken place in the USSR over the last 60 years. The struggle has been three-way, not two-way ('between capital and labour'). When the profound crises of 1928–33, 1941–44 and 1945–48 shook Soviet society and the power of the bureaucracy, on every occasion the bureaucracy struck simultaneously at both the bourgeoisie and the working class. It did the same in Eastern Europe. It did not simply 'overexploit the working class', it also expropriated the bourgeoisie. Historically it has played an autonomous role.

The real theoretical debate turns on the extent of this relative autonomy and how long it can last. For believers in the theory of 'bureaucratic collectivism', this autonomy is identical with that of a ruling class in history. For Trotsky, as for us, it is much more limited, both in time and scope. But that does not make it any the less genuine, much more genuine than the majority of Marxists thought possible before 1927. To persist in ignoring this today is to deprive oneself of an explanation of what has actually happened in the USSR since then.

The fourth great crisis in the history of the bureaucratized USSR is now unfolding. It remains to be seen whether the three-way struggle continues (we think it will), or whether, as many commentators and tendencies believe, the *nomenklatura* will go over into the camp of the international bourgeoisie lock, stock and barrel and become its resident junior partner (very junior: look at the GDR!).

Be that as it may, ends and means have to be clearly distinguished in this complex social struggle: what the fundamental driving force is, what means are used to fulfil the ends chosen, and what the objective results are of the interaction between ends and means. And here we are forced to return to the conclusion – a conclusion moreover which corresponds to Marx's definition – that only under the lash of competition has the bourgeoisie a permanent and lasting stake in the continuous expansion of production. Without this constant pressure, no pre-capitalist ruling class showed any such tendency (nor, we would add, does the bureaucratic caste in the USSR).

As long as the shortage of consumption goods kept them thirsty for more, the bureaucrats were fanatical about accumulation, about 'production for the sake of production' and about 'technological progress' (as sections of the middle bureaucracy, in their greed for an American yuppie lifestyle, still are today). But as soon as the *nomenklatura* as a whole had reached a satisfactory level of consumption ('when socialism had been achieved for its benefit') this thirst began to disappear. 'Productivist fanaticism' dwindled. A stage of what the Hungarian Stalinist ex-prime minister, Hegedüs, correctly called 'generalized irresponsibility' set in.

This also explains why Soviet managers, unlike their capitalist counterparts, nearly always and almost automatically give in to wage demands in the workplace: no pressure of competition forces them to 'extract the maximum surplus value' from the workers. The only pressure they are under is to 'avoid problems' when it comes to fulfilling the plan. It is in order to bring about a thorough change in their attitude that Gorbachev and his ilk have been trying to introduce all the technocratic changes of *Perestroika*. However, as the most consistent supporters of *Perestroika* and of out and out 'economic liberalisation', both East and West, have clearly understood, radical 'structural reform' cannot be fulfilled without a massive return to private property.

Without competition and the drive to private accumulation which it sets in motion the behaviour of the bureaucrats in the East will in essence never be like that of capitalist bosses. At best they will act like gangsters trying to legalise theft and extortion ('trying to go legit'). And if they embark on all out privatisation, which would mean making tens of millions of people unemployed in the USSR, they will have to break the resistance of the working class.

This proves that a genuine 'three-way struggle' is still taking place in the USSR. It proves that, despite everything, workers still have at least two 'gains' from the October revolution to defend: more than half a century of uninterrupted full employment (which has never existed in capitalist society and never will exist); and the abolition of private property in large scale production, without which this full employment cannot be achieved.

By dogmatically and unrealistically defining the bureaucracy as a 'capitalist class' the SWP comrades are unable to grasp what is specific about the Soviet bureaucracy. The bureaucracy differs from the bourgeois class, indeed from all ruling classes in history, by virtue of the fact that the income of those classes (its portion of the social product) is variable, while that of the bureaucrats is fixed. The annual profits of the bourgeoisie depend on the annual fluctuations in profit and production. The annual feudal rent depended on annual fluctuations in the harvests. The annual income of the bureaucrat depends on his (or her) position in the hierarchy. If that position does not change, the income does not change either, except marginally.

Hence the conservatism, inertia and 'irresponsibility' of the bureaucracy in stark contrast to the behaviour of the capitalist entrepreneur. The latter behaves differently not because he is 'more aggressive' or 'more rational', 'better' or 'worse' than the bureaucrat, or more of an 'individualist.' He does so because capitalist competition means that the struggle over the distribution of the mass of surplus value and profit is never eliminated, which means his share of it can never be guaranteed. If he slips up on the path of 'technological progress' or of 'labour organization' the inevitable consequence will be a fall in his share, if not bankruptcy.

Nothing of what *Glasnost* has come to reveal about the reality of the Soviet economy has had any light shed on it by the myths of 'state capitalism', myths which are only the reverse side of the Stalinist coin about the 'achievements of socialist industrialisation.' All can be explained in the light of the analysis made by Trotsky and the Fourth International of Soviet society and the Soviet economy, and of the analysis underpinning it of the specific nature of the Soviet bureaucracy.

Harman claims that nowhere in history has a section of the producing class been involved in the 'maximum extraction of surplus labour' from the producers themselves. Without doubt, the Soviet bureaucracy is an unprecedented phenomenon historically. But the October revolution and the creation of the isolated Russian workers' state were also new phenomena lacking historical precedent (the Paris Commune lasted only a few months). People with a scientific and undogmatic outlook should not be surprised if a new historical development throws up new and unexpected by-products.

Let us turn to the question of 'maximum extraction of surplus labour.' The proportion of working-class consumption in the USSR is much bigger than in Brazil, to take just one example of a country engaged in accelerated industrialisation (not that of working class and middle class consumption put together: the middle classes consume ten times more than workers and account for 20 per cent of the population).

Let us call to mind a simple analogy (which is not to say it is identical, just analogous). For any socialist or trade unionist in 1848 or 1890 the idea of socialist party leaders or reactionary trade union leaders acting so as to objectively increase the 'extraction of surplus labour from the producers' would have appeared literally unthinkable. Yet that is what social democratic leaders have done since 1914, and a good number of trade union leaders since even before that date. Should one therefore refuse to call social democratic parties workers' parties? Have they become bourgeois parties, identical with the Conservatives and the Liberals? Is it possible to engage in class politics in Europe or Japan without having to defend these parties against the bourgeoisie's attempts to weaken or even periodically crush them?

Must the mass trade unions under the leadership of reformist traitors be considered as yellow bosses' unions? The ultralefts have long defended this absurd idea, which the SWP comrades reject as far as Great Britain is concerned. But why, if it is conceivable to defend the SPD against fascism, despite its being led by the Noskes, the assassins of Karl Liebknecht and Rosa Luxemburg, is it 'inconceivable' to defend the USSR against imperialism?

Chris Harman claims that two arguments we successively put forward about the bureaucracy are mutually incompatible. The first is that the bureaucracy is not a ruling class; the second is that it controls and distributes the bulk of the social surplus in the USSR. But this incompatibility yet again reflects a formalist, schematic and simplistically dogmatic manner of thinking.

There have been many cases in history where powerful social layers controlled and distributed the bulk of the surplus despite not being the ruling class. For to be a ruling class involves appropriating the surplus, which is not necessarily the same as controlling or distributing it. The mandarins at the height of the Chinese Empire and the imperial bureaucracy in the late Roman Empire were by and large in control of the centralization and distribution of the social surplus. But for all that they were not the ruling classes in these two societies, because they did not appropriate the major share of the surplus. At the end of the Third Reich, the Nazi military bureaucracy certainly controlled the distribution of what was produced socially. But it was in no sense the ruling class, since the bulk of the social surplus continued to be appropriated by the capitalist class. The events which followed showed who was master and who, despite the appearance of omnipotence, only carried out orders.

Future events will similarly demonstrate that the Soviet bureaucracy will only be able to become a ruling class by appropriating to itself the social surplus and the means of production, that is to say, by turning into 'old fashioned' capitalists who own a good chunk of the large scale means of production.

A fear that has proved groundless
When he decided to break with the interpretation of Soviet society formulated by Trotsky and defended by the Fourth International, Tony Cliff predicted that those who continued to call the USSR a bureaucratically degenerated workers' state would be led to capitulate to Stalinism, in particular to side with the bureaucracy against workers in revolt. (Incidentally,

let us recall that as early as Stalin's death, if not from 1948 onwards, we predicted such revolts.)

Subsequent events have proved this prediction to be groundless. Neither the Fourth International, nor any of its sections, nor any of its leading representatives, has even once lined up 'on the side of the bureaucracy against the masses in revolt.' We all gave 100 per cent support to the workers' uprising in the GDR in 1953, to the 1956 Hungarian revolution, to the Polish workers' struggles in the same year, to the Prague Spring's resistance in 1968–69 to the Soviet invasion, to the rise of *Solidarnosć* in 1980–81 and to its subsequent struggle against Jaruzelski's military coup in Poland, and to the uprisings in China and Eastern Europe in 1989.

Chris Harman recognizes this, moreover. In embarrassment he falls back on the assertion that we nevertheless might have expressed a 'preference' for the Gomulka style method of reform in 1956 to that of the Hungarian revolution. This is slander. Harman will not be able to find a single quotation to back up his accusation. We have been supporters of a political revolution – a revolution involving large scale independent mass action and self-organization – ever since we began to take part in debates on the 'nature of the USSR' (i.e., since 1945–6), and remain so. We have never budged an inch from this position. But the reality of the political mass struggles in the USSR, Eastern Europe and like societies cannot be reduced to struggles between the masses and the bureaucracy.

In the USSR, Eastern Europe, China, Cuba and Nicaragua, the struggles of the last 50 years have also taken place between, on the one hand, these states and the masses in these countries and, on the other, the imperialist powers. The theory of state capitalism has been no kind of guide in these conflicts, to say the least. Its internal logic would necessarily lead one to view most of these conflicts as inter-imperialist and take an absentionist, 'third camp' position (which is what Cliff adopted in the Korean War and which at least some of his followers were tempted to do in the Bay of Pigs conflict). It is true that during the Vietnamese War he took a more correct position, but one in flagrant contradiction to the logic of the theory of 'state capitalism.'

In these conflicts the popular masses of those countries, starting with the workers, did not remain neutral. They lined up against imperialism, despite their hatred of Stalin and his heirs. In practice they applied Trotsky's line of military defence of the USSR (and the other bureaucratized workers' states) against imperialism. They did so in the USSR, in Yugoslavia, in China, in Vietnam, in Cuba and in Nicaragua. In these confrontations, which involved tens of millions of workers, the attitude adopted by the few followers of the theory of 'state capitalism' was at best confused and contradictory, at worst plainly counterrevolutionary. If Soviet workers had had the misfortune to follow these false guides, none of us would be alive today and no independent workers' organization would exist in Europe, if not in other continents. The triumph of Nazi barbarism would have destroyed them.

The vicious circle of sectarianism

The tendency led by Tony Cliff (from which the SWP came) has seen its main task ever since its birth as spreading the theory of 'state capitalism.' This is the characteristic mark of a sect as defined by Marx: in order to justify its existence, it constructs a shibboleth out of a particular doctrine and subordinates its activity to the defence of that shibboleth.

This sectarian deviation has its own logic from which it is almost impossible to escape. In Britain itself the SWP comrades have been partially protected from the worst sins of sectarianism because of their real roots in the working class and because of the size of their organization: any type of irresponsible behaviour is impossible when acting under the critical gaze of thousands. But even in Britain the sectarian frame of mind has damaged and continues to damage the SWP, particularly in its approach to those mass movements which it considers 'non-proletarian' and carelessly dubs 'petty bourgeois.' This derives from the same inability to grasp the notion of combined development which arises as a transitional phenomenon, particularly in the sphere of class consciousness. It is the same 'all or nothing' attitude which lies at the heart of the theory of 'state capitalism.'

Sectarianism has especially damaged the SWP's international work in another way. The theory of state capitalism means that it is powerless to grasp the full progressive dynamic of the mass anti-imperialist movements in the Third World. According to that theory, these movements can only lead in the end to the creation of new state capitalist states. Their dynamic is a purely 'nationalistic' one. The entire strategy of permanent revolution – total support for the anti-imperialist struggle while fighting for the political class independence of the proletariat; a struggle for proletarian hegemony inside the movement; striving to ensure that in solving its national-democratic tasks the revolution grows over into making a start on solving its socialist-proletarian ones – is in fact rejected or minimalised by the leadership of the SWP.

In other imperialist countries besides Britain, the followers of the SWP mostly content themselves with forming grouplets to propagate the theory of state capitalism, which are incapable, if only because of their tiny size, of intervening in genuine class struggle. Sectarian interests take precedence over class interests. The same applies in the states of Eastern Europe, which are in complete social and political turmoil. In the *Communist Manifesto* Marx and Engels provided the classic definition of what communists have to do:

> *They have no interests separate and apart from those of the proletariat as a whole. They do not set up any special principles [in the 1888 English edition Engels preferred to insert 'sectarian principles'] of their own, by which to shape and mould the proletarian movement.*

> *The communists are distinguished from the other working-class parties by this only: 1) In the national struggles of the proletarians of the different countries, they point out and bring to the front the common interests of the entire proletariat, independently of all nationality. 2) In the various stages of development which the struggle of the working class against the bourgeoisie has to pass through,*

they always and everywhere represent the interests of the movement as a whole.

The Communists, therefore, are on the one hand, practically, the most advanced and resolute section of the working class parties of every country, that section which pushes forward all others; on the other hand, theoretically, they have over the great mass of the proletariat the advantage of clearly understanding the line of march, the conditions, and the ultimate general results of the proletarian movement.

The SWP is no different from the Fourth International when it comes to 'understanding the line of march, the conditions, and the ultimate general results of the proletarian movement' in Eastern Europe and the USSR: the proletariat organizes itself to conquer power through multiparty, democratically elected Soviets, with the perspective of constructing a classless society internationally.

But the followers of the SWP do not draw the obvious conclusion that a separate organization of state caps is unjustified in these Eastern European countries. They do not see that the task of any revolutionary there is to help advanced workers and intellectuals battle on two fronts, against the bureaucracy and against restorationist forces. Instead of defending the interests of the proletariat as a whole, which above all demands the (re)creation of class independence (no easy matter), the followers of the SWP concentrate on stirring up an artificial distinction from every other revolutionary current – a distinction exclusively based on acceptance of the dogma of 'state capitalism', their sectarian shibboleth.

That can only reinforce the image of revolutionary Marxists as scholastic dogmatists, as hopeless 'splitters', which first Stalinists and then neo-Stalinists and neo-social democrats have systematically spread in these countries in order to discredit revolutionary Marxists (and increasingly these days Marxism itself). This image is counterproductive. It weakens the real possibilities that Marxists have in these countries, not to found sects, but to become the major pole of attraction for the militant left inside the workers' movement as it reconstructs itself.

Fortunately the negative effect of this will remain limited, both because of the theoretical, political and organizational strength which the Fourth International has already gained (its influence is real there in a way that the SWP's is not), and because of the understanding and experience that the best indigenous forces springing up in those countries have progressively accumulated that the role played there by the SWP clearly illustrates the negative repercussions of sectarianism.

This sectarianism has made the SWP incapable of making any progress towards the construction of an international organization. Sects can only link up with mini-sects which they closely control. Organizationally, their sectarianism prevents them linking up with substantial, autonomous revolutionary bodies in an important number of countries. Politically, this is because they fail to understand the real process of mass struggle in most countries in the world. The SWP is essentially, then, a national-communist organization, which is forced to fob its members off by trying to create grouplets in a few countries.

After 40 years experience our record in this respect cannot be faulted. The Fourth International exists for real as the one and only world organization. It is, of course, still small, too small, and is far from being the mass revolutionary international for which it is working and of which it will constitute just one element. However, it is much stronger than in 1938 or than in 1948, both in numbers, in rootedness in the workplace and unions, and in geographical terms. It exists in 50 countries or so. Some of its sections and sympathising organizations play a genuine part in the workers' movement and the mass movement in their respective countries, which is recognized by all. It acts and will continue to act in a non-sectarian fashion, on the basis laid down above in the *Communist Manifesto*.

It can do so because it represents the one current in the international workers' movement which takes on the unconditional and uncompromising defence of the interests of the workers and the oppressed in the three sectors of the world revolution – the imperialist countries, the countries under bureaucratic dictatorship and the so called Third World countries – without anywhere subordinating this defence to any supposed 'priorities.' This is what allows the building at one and the same time of national revolutionary organizations and of an international revolutionary organization. In this respect, an understanding, based on the theory of permanent revolution, on the Trotskyist analysis of Stalinism, on *The Transitional Programme* and on the 'dialectic of the three sectors of the world revolution', of what has happened, and is happening in the USSR, in the Third World and in the organized workers' movement in the imperialist countries, has proved both operational and effective.

Criticism which does not withstand the test of logic

Chris Harman

The coincidence of economic crises East and West present revolutionary Marxists with a great challenge. The old Stalinist ideology which dominated so much of the workers' movement in the West and the Third World has collapsed. Its collapse has left a vacuum which the opponents of Marxism and of class politics are trying to fill with claims that 'the market' offers the only way forward for humanity. Such claims receive encouragement from the reaction of very large numbers of workers in the countries of the former Eastern bloc to the economic crisis that besets them: believing the old order to be some variant of socialism they themselves reject talk of socialism and turn towards people like Walesa or Yeltsin who preach the wonders of Western capitalism.

There is only one way for revolutionary socialists to meet this challenge. It is to provide an analysis of the world system which shows the interaction between crisis in the East and crisis in the West. Unfortunately, Ernest Mandel fails to do this.

His account of modern Western capitalism is simplistic in the extreme. He presents us with a precis of what he claims was Marx's account 120 years ago in *Capital*. He tells us that under modern capitalism:

> *The organization of labour depends in the first place on the private decisions of the factory owner, which are then corrected by competition, by the market. He has to submit to these corrections or face extinction. Under capitalism there is only one measure of performance – profit ... It is post-sales profits that determine everything. The capitalist economy is based on profits, and profit can only be realised and measured in the form of money. Capitals move out of enterprises and sectors below average profit into those of above average profit ...*
>
> *At the first sign of a loss or of below average profits he (the capitalist) attempts to change the way production is organized... The law of value only rules any economy insofar as it is one of generalized commodity production, that is, one in which labour is basically private labour.*

This account is not, of course, completely wrong. But it is hopelessly inadequate when it comes to dealing with the empirical reality of the system since Marx's time. To deal with that you cannot simply talk in terms of 'private decisions' made by the 'factory owner.' You have to analyse what happens as monopolies come to dominate the national economy, when there is the nationalization of productive sectors of the economy, when 'peaceful' competition for markets gives way to military conflict between capitalist states, when states override the workings of the law of value inside their economies so as to ensure expansion of the sectors vital for military success.

It was precisely these issues which Lenin and Bukharin began to confront with their writings on imperialism.[107] Their writings took for granted Marx's account in *Capital*, but saw the need to build on it. Far from simply talking about 'competition for markets' they recognized that capitalism was beginning to go beyond this stage of its history (already, in 1915 and 1916!). Mandel, by contrast, is content to stick with his summary of Marx, without even referring to what Lenin and Bukharin wrote 75 years ago!

If that is not enough, he dismisses out of hand those of us who have attempted to build on their insights for accepting 'the myth' of 'organized capitalism' and Hilferding's *Generalkartel.* Yet Engels could write, more than a century ago:

When we move on to the trusts which control and monopolise whole branches [of industry] then that means an end not only to private production but also to planlessness.[108]

Presumably, he too accepted 'the myth of organized capitalism.' Presumably Lenin did also, when he wrote a very favourable introduction to Bukharin's *Imperialism and the World Economy,* with its insistence (already in 1915) that, 'Competition is reduced to a minimum within the boundaries of 'national economies'' but 'flares up in colossal proportion' as 'the struggle between state capitalist trusts', a struggle which 'is decided in the first place by the relation between their military forces.'[109] Finally, presumably Trotsky made the same mistake when he wrote, in *The Manifesto of the Communist International to the Workers of the World:*

The statisation of economic life, against which the capitalist liberalism used to protest so much, has become an accomplished fact ... It is impossible to return not only to free competition but even to the domination of trusts, syndicates and other economic octopuses. Today the one and only issue is: Who shall here forth be the bearer of statised production – the imperialist state or the victorious proletariat?[110]

Lenin, Bukharin and Trotsky all recognized that once capitalism enters its monopoly, imperialist, phase it is dominated by gigantic concerns which certainly do not organize the processes of production inside them on the basis of exchange of commodities at market prices, but by a planned interaction of inputs and outputs. It is something of which those who today run the giant corporations are only too aware. So a recent account of the workings of South Korea's giant *chaebol* conglomerates can tell:

The performance of Korea's big businesses cannot be measured by profitability, because profit data are manipulated, nor can it be measured by volume of exports, which may merely reflect subsidisation. Good performance must be measured by physical indicators of production and operations management – say, productivity, quality and inventories, as well as changes in export values.[111]

Inside the firm there is a form of 'planning', often running counter to the relations between commodities which would follow from the law of value.

What is true inside the giant firm is just as true inside the enormous military sectors of modern states – which during the two world wars came to dominate virtually the whole of each national economy. Even when the state does not produce arms directly, it ensures that private contractors are paid on a 'cost plus' basis, thus keeping them in business regardless of whether this involves subsidising unprofitable sectors of the economy at the expense of more profitable ones. No modern state allows the internal workings of the market – of the law of value – to destroy its ability to wage war.

But this is not the end of the matter. The law of value which is banished from the internal operation of the giant corporation or the military preparations of the state, nevertheless exercises a vital determining force on them from the outside. The direction which this 'planning' takes is not an arbitrary one. It has to enable each giant concern to compete with others – in military or economic terms – in the long run.

A giant corporation which cannot make an overall profit on the sum total of its transactions, profitable and unprofitable combined, will eventually go out of business. A national state which does not use its resources in such a way as to enable it to outshoot its rivals will eventually risk military defeat.

External competition determines the parameters according to which the 'planners' inside each concern operate. It is this external competition which forces managements to worry continually about their internal production costs, that is, to try to impose the law of value on the various production processes under their control.

But, of course, the vagaries of external competition continually make nonsense of the attempt at internal planning, upsetting old cost calculations, compelling managements to enlarge certain production facilities much more than was 'planned' and to leave others half finished. Attempts at 'organization' within the national economy are continually disrupted by competition at the international level. And that does not just mean economic competition for markets. It also means the form of competition typical of the epoch of imperialism, military competition.

Mandel's myths about the East

Mandel's mythical account of the functioning of modern Western capitalism is followed by a mythical account of what has happened inside the Eastern states. He argues that:

> *In the USSR the key essential investments are not distributed by the law of value. They are decided by the bureaucracy, mostly at state level. It is a planned economy, planned as far as direct allocation of resources is concerned. For 70 years, loss making enterprises required large subsidies and have received preferential allocation of productive resources. These have been systematically diverted from 'more profitable' enterprises or sectors. Such phenomena are unthinkable under capitalism and the law of value.*

So it was that 'from 1928 onwards ... growth really was regular and uninterrupted ... unlike the capitalist economy, the USSR has experienced no recession, no crisis of overproduction leading to an absolute fall in production from more than half a century.' Finally, although 'the rate of growth began to fall about 20 years ago' and 'this fall may become 'zero growth' ... there is no law making it inevitable.'

If there is a dynamic in the economy of the USSR, he argues, it is certainly not the one to which the theory of state capitalism points, of accumulation of means of production, since much of this accumulation turns out to be waste goods. 'Here we have the secret of the command economy: it is Department III which is over expanded, not Department I.'

This is proved, he claims, by the way the USSR's agriculture is so unsuccessful, although 'the USSR is the biggest producer of chemical fertiliser in the world', producing 'nearly as much as the USA and Western Europe put together.' Apparently 'more than half the fertiliser is lost in transit.' 'Such wastage has nothing to do … with any drive to accumulate capital.'

Let's look at each of his claims in turn. First, the claim that growth has been 'regular and uninterrupted' is refuted by the most perceptive East European economists. They long ago recognized that the development of the Stalinist command economies has been cyclical in character, repeatedly creating crisis situations. And the fluctuations in the course of the cycles have often been greater than those which the Western economies experienced during the long boom of the 1950s and 1960s. As the Czechoslovak economists Goldman and Korba told in 1969:

> *Analysis of the dynamics of industrial production in Czechoslovakia, the German Democratic Republic and Hungary supplies an interesting picture. The rate of growth shows relatively regular fluctuations … These fluctuations are even more pronounced if analysis is confined to producer goods.*[112]

These fluctuations were substantially greater for Czechoslovakia in the 1950s and 1960s than for France. In the period 1966–74, the difference between growth rates in minimum growth years and maximum growth years averaged 50 per cent for East Germany, 100 per cent for Bulgaria, 130 per cent for the USSR and 228 per cent for Poland.

A Western academic study 20 years ago, showed that such unevenness was already visible in the Soviet Union at the time of the First Five Year plan.[113] We now know, from post-*Perestroika* Soviet accounts, that the massive expansion of industrial output in the early plan years led in 1932–33 to an exhaustion of food supplies and a famine which killed more than 5 million people, mostly in the Ukraine and Kazakhstan.

What is more recession – negative growth – was not completely ruled out in the way that Mandel claims: it occurred in Yugoslavia in 1951–52 and 1967, and in Czechoslovakia in the early 1960s. And it is occurring in the USSR today (October 1990), *before* reforms intended to introduce Western style market mechanisms.

In the early 1970s the Yugoslav economist Branko Horvat was able to publish a book called *Business Cycles in Yugoslavia*[114] which pointed out that even before the market reforms of 1968, the Yugoslav economy was 'significantly more unstable' than ten other economies that were cited, 'including the United States.'[115] The very title of the book should have been an impossibility according to Mandel.

Today, of course, Mandel no longer repeats his old claim that crises cannot occur in the Eastern states: he can hardly assert that the whole Russian leadership are wrong when they point to such a thing. But he does still insist:

> *If there is a crisis ... it is one of underproduction of use values (of scarcity) and not of overproduction of exchange values (of commodities). To claim that the first is only a variant of the second is a gross fallacy. An empty shop is not 'a variant' of a shop stuffed with unsellable goods.*

It simply is not good enough to assert that because two things are opposites they can have no connection with each other. As a Marxist, Mandel should understand that much. In fact, 'overproduction' is, according to Marx's analysis, only one moment in the development of the internal contradictions of capitalism. That is why Marxists could continue to insist on the reality of these contradictions throughout the long boom when generalized crises of overproduction did not materialise in many Western countries.[116]

As Marx points out in volume III of *Capital*, overproduction of commodities is a by-product of something else – overproduction of capital. But this is not some absolute overproduction in relation to the needs of society – which can always be expanded and, in fact, are never fully satisfied when 'overproduction' arises. It is overproduction of capital – overaccumulation – in relation to the surplus value being pumped from the workforce.

Marx spells out how overproduction comes about. At a certain point in any boom the competitive drive of capitalists to invest leads to a drying up of existing supplies of raw materials, labour and loanable capital (i.e., non-invested surplus value). The prices of all these things – commodity prices, money wages and interest rates – begin to rise until the least profitable firms suddenly find they are operating at a loss. Some go out of business. Others survive, but only by abandoning planned investments and closing down factories. Their actions in turn destroy markets for other capitals, forcing them to abandon investments and close down factories. The 'excess demand' (Mandel's 'underproduction') of the boom gives rise to the overproduction of the slump. But the slump, in turn, prepares the way for a new boom by raising the proportion of surplus value to capital: on the one hand, some capitals are driven out of business reducing the total stock of capital; on the other, slump conditions allow capitalists to increase the rate of exploitation and to enter a new cycle of accumulation with a greater amount of surplus value.

The secret of the Western long boom of the 1940s, 1950s and 1960s lay in the way the national state could reduce the pressures leading to over-accumulation (by diverting a portion of capital into non-productive, military channels), take direct action to try to maintain a high rate of exploitation (through wage controls etc.), intervene to slow down the boom before it led key firms to become unprofitable and maintain a minimum guaranteed level of demand through military orders. The state monopoly capitalist arms economy was not able to do away with the cyclical pattern of capitalist accumulation. But it was able to prevent it leading to slumps of the pre-Second World War sort.

The situation was very similar with the Stalinist command economies of the Eastern states. As in Marx's picture of capitalism there was over-accumulation. The attempt to compete with bigger and more advanced foreign capitalisms led to a scale of investment in excess of the surplus available within the national economy. And the overaccumulation led to a cyclical pattern of development, involving crisis. Attempting an excessive level of investment inevitably led to growing shortages of raw materials, intermediate components and labour.

Bottlenecks arose throughout the economy, threatening the closure of vast sectors of production through shortages of inputs. Output never rose nearly as rapidly as planned. The monetary funds paid out by enterprises for materials and labour exceeded the output of the economy, giving rise to inflationary pressures which found direct expression as price rises or 'hidden' expression as acute shortages of goods in the shops.

Left to itself, the crisis of excess demand – the product of excess accumulation – would eventually have spilled over into the wholesale closure of enterprises and the destruction of the markets for the output of other enterprises. It would have become a crisis of overproduction of commodities. But as in the West in the long boom, the state stepped in to try and pre-empt this by 'cooling down' the economy. It ordered enterprises to 'freeze' certain investments and to divert resources to others. This involved factories suddenly switching from one sort of output to another. The myth of the pre-planning of production – a myth which Mandel still accepts when he speaks of 'a priori allocation' – gave way to the reality of after the event, 'a posteriori', allocation, with a repeated shifting of inputs and outputs.

One plan target which always suffered in the process was that for consumer goods production. Directly cutting into 'wage fund goods' released resources for completing other investments. The balance between investment and surplus value was restored, in part, by physically limiting consumption levels so as to raise the rate of exploitation. The result, of course, was to increase still further the discrepancy between the funds laid out by enterprises on wages and the goods available for these wages to buy – to increase open or hidden inflation.

Overall, the economy was subject to periodic crises, even if these did not express themselves exactly in accordance with Marx's model.

But that is not the end of the matter. Mandel is wrong in his second contention, that there was even growth until '20 years ago.' In fact, all the Eastern economies suffered for decades from a long-term trend for average growth rates to decline. And this was not, as Mandel claims, something which only became visible in the course of the 1960s. Official USSR figures give the following growth rates:

Average annual growth of national income produced

1951–55	11.3 per cent
1956–60	9.2 per cent
1961–65	6.5 per cent
1966–70	7.8 per cent
1971–75	5.7 per cent

Other authoritative estimates show lower average growth rates, but the same trend.[117]

The difficulty in attaining the old rates of growth were certainly clear to the Soviet leaders as early as December 1956 when, for the first time, they abandoned a peace time 'plan' for being 'too taut', that is, for setting impossible investment targets. As one of the standard Western academic works on the Soviet economy notes, 'a slowdown in growth became quite noticeable after 1958.'[118]

Khrushchev's repeated and unsuccessful attempts to reorganize the economy in the mid-1950s and early 1960s (his 'hare brained schemes', as they were called in the Brezhnev years) arose precisely because of these economic failings. Yet Mandel's theory led him to deny the reality of such failings at the time, and leads him now to claim that it was not until '20 years ago' (i.e., in 1970, not the mid-1950s) did 'the rate of growth began to fall'!

By contrast, whether Mandel was aware of it or not, Tony Cliff's theory did enable him in the mid-1950s to locate the economic problems behind Khrushchev's failures.[119]

When it comes to the present, Mandel's claims are even more amazing. He tells us that although the decline in Soviet growth rates 'may become zero growth ... there is no law making it inevitable.' In fact, while he was writing these words in the early summer of 1989, there was already not just 'zero growth' in the USSR, but the beginning of a sharp decline in total output. By October 1990 Tolkushin, the deputy chairman of the USSR state committee for statistics, was announcing, 'During September, by comparison with September of last year, industrial output was down by 3.1 per cent.'[120]

The question Marxists have to be able to answer is how this economic contraction came about. And it is not good enough to try to duck that question by saying it was 'not inevitable.' That is to put yourself in a no better position than apologists for Western capitalism who claim that recessions are 'not inevitable' but just a result of mistakes in economic policy, without saying from where those mistakes come.

Mandel's claim that there cannot be accumulation because there is waste, is amazing. He would have us think there is not great waste in the West! In fact, calculations of waste in the West, whether by muck rakers of the Vance Packard school, by Baran and Sweezy[121] or by Mike Kidron[122] suggest that it exceeds the 30 or 40 per cent of available productive resources' of which Mandel talks in the case of the USSR.

The claim that the USSR is a uniquely wasteful economy has long come from a group of theorists around the magazine *Critique*. They hold that the USSR is neither socialist nor capitalist. More recently, it has been taken up by many East European economists and political leaders who see it as justifying a turn towards an untrammelled market model which, they believe, exists in the West.

But, as Mandel himself used to recognize (in debate with *Critique* editor Hillel Ticktin), it is not a contention that can stand up to even the most cursory historical examination of the Soviet economy. For between the late 1920s and the 1960s the USSR did 'catch up' with the Western economies sufficiently to become the world's second economic power. It could not have done so if it was only the waste sector of the economy, Department III, which grew.

In fact, as every serious study of the USSR has concluded, there was massive growth of the means of production, of Department I. The ability of the USSR to defeat Nazi Germany and then to match the US in the arms race (at least until recently) was testimony to this: although things like tanks, atomic submarines and nuclear missiles are part of Department III, they cannot be produced unless there exists a huge, productive, heavy industrial sector. And that requires a massive accumulation of means of production, a massive growth of Department I.

What is more, Mandel is completely wrong to say such accumulation could not be the cause of waste. The forced growth of heavy industry in the Stalin years could only take place because other sectors of the economy, especially those providing for the living standards of workers, were systematically robbed of resources. So under Stalinist 'collectivisation' there was a very low level of investment in agriculture, and those who worked the land did so for minimal wages. They survived mainly on the potatoes they grew on their own dwarf private plots, while the state took from them virtually all the grain to feed a burgeoning industrial workforce in the cities – and in the worst famine years of the 1930s, to export to pay for machinery imports.

In the first two decades after Stalin's death there were repeated attempts to improve the situation in agriculture, but every increase in military tension with the US led to a diversion of resources to heavy industry and armaments and away from rural investment.

Khrushchev's failure to improve agricultural output substantially was an important factor in bringing about his fall in 1964. Yet those who overthrew him were unable to pour the resources into agriculture which they at first promised: tractor and truck output in 1970 was only about half that laid down in the 1966–70 'plan', while fertiliser output was about 30 per cent under target.[123] As Brezhnev's statisticians explained:

Owing to the international situation it has not been possible to allocate as many resources as intended to agricultural investment and whilst the 1969 figure exceeds that for 1968, it is below that envisaged in the directives for 1966–70.[124]

The cumulative result of the low level of agricultural investment was a continual haemorrhage of young workers from the countryside until it was populated mainly by old people, and a failure to build an infrastructure of roads, storage equipment and so forth. So even when the regime did, out of desperation, boost agriculture after the grain crisis of 1972, it lacked both the skilled, motivated workforce needed to take advantage of the most modern methods and the facilities for shifting the crop in the years when there was a good harvest.[125]

And once *détente* gave way in 1979–80 to the second Cold War, agricultural investment was again sacrificed for industry and the arms budget: the capital stock in agriculture grew faster than that in industry between 1971–80, only to fall behind again in 1981–86.[126]

Mandel's example of fertiliser illustrates the point very well. The diversion of resources from investment in fertiliser plants to heavy industry meant that in 1968 Soviet agriculture was using only 62 kilogramme of fertiliser per hectare, as against 227 kilogramme per hectare in the US and 766 per hectare in Britain.

Of course, waste contributed to the low Soviet level, but it was not the *main* cause. And what is more, the waste itself could be a by-product of the forced accumulation – as when the pressure to switch resources to 'priority' heavy industrial projects prevented the completion of a factory which was due to produce bags to carry increased fertiliser output, leading to much of it going to waste.[127]

Today, 20 years on, total mineral fertiliser consumption has indeed overtaken the US figure, as Mandel states. But he is grossly ill informed if he believes it is 'nearly as much' as that of 'the USA and West Europe put together.' Soviet consumption in 1986 was 23.08 million tonnes, combined US and Western European consumption 41.07 million tonnes.[128] The amount of fertiliser per hectare of arable land is only slightly higher than the US figure, although the innate average fertility of US land is considerably higher than that of Soviet land (although there is about the same amount of arable land in the USSR as the US, most of it lies in more northerly latitudes) and much Soviet fertiliser is low grade.[129] But, most significantly, low levels of agricultural investment mean there are 40 per cent fewer tractors in the USSR than the US, making it much more difficult to transport and spread fertiliser without wastage.[130]

So inferior fertiliser is used on less fertile land by a workforce which has lost most of its younger, skilled members to the towns and heavy industry. And that fertiliser has to be distributed by an inadequate tractor fleet across a vast area of countryside lacking even the most minimal investment in roads and storage facilities. It is not surprising that Soviet agriculture remains much less productive and much more wasteful than that in the US. But you cannot see why unless you recognize the way in which the economy as a whole is dominated by the drive to accumulate.

But Mandel does not just accept fashionable 'new class theorist' arguments about waste. He also repeats arguments which used to be the basis of Stalinist apologetics for the Eastern states.

So he claims that 'unemployment has played no role in the USSR for more than half a century.' This 'gain from the October revolution' is something 'which has never existed in capitalist society and never will.' Yet the Soviet press has admitted in the last year to high levels of structural unemployment in whole regions of the USSR. *Pravda* has told that in 1986 there was 27.6 per cent unemployment in Azerbaijan and 18 per cent in Armenia[131] and *Moscow News* has spoken of 6 million unemployed in the Asiatic republics.[132] Even in its early, centrally directed version, *Perestroika* included the sacking of workers by technologically backward factories. So a spring 1990 estimate by *Izvestia* of total Soviet unemployment of 8 million could be correct[133] – even though it would mean an unemployment rate in the USSR similar to that in a Western capitalist country like the US[134] and considerably greater than that of Japan!

More incredibly, Mandel claims that 'the proportion of working-class consumption in the USSR' is 'much bigger' than in other countries with a similar level of economic development. In fact, it was possible last year for one of the heads of the official, state run unions to declare that 'the proportion of the wages' fund of workers and office workers in the country's national income, at 35 per cent, is considered one of the world's lowest.'[135] He may have been exaggerating. But if Mandel is going to claim the proportion of workers consumption is 'much bigger' than in comparable countries elsewhere in the world, he had better provide some evidence.

Even more astonishing, however, than Mandel's propensity to indulge in apologetics that even the Stalinists themselves have abandoned, is his ability to contradict himself over something which is central to his whole understanding of how the Soviet economy has functioned. 'We have never defended the thesis', he writes, 'that the economic development of the USSR is dominated by the production of consumption goods for the bureaucracy.' Yet only two paragraphs later he argues:

> In order to preserve and extend its privileges the Soviet bureaucracy ... has to develop the economy up to a certain point ... Without car factories 3 million middle and top bureaucrats cannot acquire cars. Without enough steel, electricity or iron ore, the car industry cannot be developed satisfactorily.

If this is not saying that the bureaucracy's need for consumption goods is the driving force of the economy, what is it saying?

He then goes on to see this drive for bureaucratic consumption as responsible for both the fast rate of economic growth under Stalin and its slower growth more recently:

> For as long as the shortage of consumption goods kept them thirsty for more, the bureaucrats were fanatical about accumulation, about 'production for the sake of production' and about 'technological progress.' But as soon as the nomenklatura as a whole had reached a satisfactory level of consumption, this thirst began to disappear.

I can only explain such contradictory utterances in one way. Mandel momentarily grasped the stupidity of trying to explain in terms of the consumption needs of the bureaucracy an economy, like the Soviet one, characterized by a massive tendency for heavy industry to expand. But then he slipped back into his old explanations, for the only rational alternative would have been to locate the drive to accumulate in terms of competition with the West. That would have driven him to accept the contentions of the theory of state capitalism. He preferred to contradict himself than to travel that path!

There is a close connection between Mandel's theoretical starting point and his factual errors. Because he refuses to recognize the fundamental forces behind economic development in the past, Mandel cannot grasp the scale of exploitation of the Soviet workers, the crisis ridden cycle of economic development, the coexistence of labour shortages in parts of the USSR alongside vast pools of unemployment in other parts, the long term decline in the growth rate, and the sudden outbreak in recent years of generalized crises which have made 'inevitable' a fall in output and a catastrophic contraction of the economy.

By contrast, those of us who see the USSR as state capitalist have long recognized the way things are going. Tony Cliff *did* in 1948 locate the main factors leading the Soviet economy inexorably from the dynamism of the Stalin years to eventual economic crisis and he *did*, in the mid-1950s, spell out how this damned the Khruschevite dream of reform. I myself pointed out 15 years ago how the long-term decline in growth rates made it increasingly difficult for state planners to resolve the cyclical crises caused by overaccumulation.[136]

It became more and more difficult for the state planners to find the resources needed to overcome bottlenecks in the economy. Growing sectors of the economy simply could not get the inputs they needed to turn out goods for which there was demand; other sectors produced goods which were stockpiled on a massive scale, since they were intended as inputs for investments that had been abandoned. 'Underproduction' in certain sectors of the economy (particularly 'wage goods' sectors) was accompanied by 'overproduction' in other sectors (particularly certain 'capital goods' sectors). The central planners could no longer prevent a physical decline in output and open inflation on a massive scale. This point was already reached in Poland in 1979–80 and has now been passed in the USSR, Bulgaria and Romania as well.

Those who ran the economy were driven to try to deal with bottlenecks by turning to the international economy. Cyclical crises in East Europe always led to foreign trade deficits as well as to inflationary trends. And in the 1970s Poland and Hungary turned to the world economy on a massive scale, seeking funds from the West for accumulation and expecting to repay them by sales on Western markets. In the 1980s the USSR and Bulgaria responded to internal crisis by beginning to move in the same direction, on a scale that has only become clear with official revelations over the last year.

But even if the turn to the international market provides temporary relief from the internal crisis (as it did in Poland in the early Gierek years, 1971–75), this soon gives way to aggravation of the crisis. The bureaucracy has to cope with the ups and downs of the world economy as well as the ups and downs of the internal economy. And the need to repay foreign debts forces the bureaucracy to worry lest the internal ratio of surplus value to investment (the rate of profit) falls below the international average.

The internal dynamic of bureaucratic state capitalism leads it into a crisis from which it tries to escape by opening itself up to the world market. But that opening reduces still further its ability to employ old mechanisms for coping with the effects of the internal crisis. Economic contractions do, indeed, become 'inevitable.'

State capitalism in the West

There is a final, very important, theoretical point that escapes Mandel's understanding. The loss of the state's ability to suppress certain symptoms of economic crisis in the last two decades is not something unique to the Eastern states. There has been similar change throughout the West and the Third World.

The merger of the state and capital had been a trend throughout the world capitalist system between the 1930s and the 1970s, of which what happened in the Eastern states was the most extreme expression. In country after country there had been, for a longer or shorter period, the direct domination by the state of whole sectors of productive industry, the growth of an enormous military sector, the subordination of much of the economy to the dictates of military competition, and the overriding of the play of market forces by state direction.

The role of the state, and of military expenditure in particular, had influenced the way in which the crisis of the system expressed itself. In looking at capitalism during the 'long boom' of the 1940s, 1950s and 1960s it had not been good enough *simply* to talk in terms of a 'crisis of overproduction' (as Mandel does). This was not the characteristic form of economic crisis in the West. In Britain, for instance, there was no generalized recession, no fall in economic output due to lack of markets, between 1940 and 1971. What occurred was 'stop-go' – repeated intervention by the state to reduce 'excess demand' ('underproduction') and to head off inflation and balance of payments deficits.

There was in those years, as Tony Cliff pointed out at the time, a great similarity between the sort of economic crisis experienced in the advanced Western states and that experienced under Stalinism:

> *It can be shown that the process that leads to contradictions in the permanent war economy – subordination of means of consumption to means of destruction, the appearance of crises of underproduction, of disproportions between branches of the economy, lack of raw materials, etc, etc – are equally applicable to Western capitalist countries and to the 'socialist' third of the world.*[137]

But all this had begun to change by the early 1970s. The state capitalist arms economy began, inevitably, to be undermined by the very economic expansion it had brought about. The forces of production began to grow beyond the bounds of national states as never before. World trade grew faster than world output, and production itself was increasingly organized internationally. Capitalists were forced to operate internationally or, at least, to link up with other capitalists internationally, if they were not to lose out in terms of technological advance and competitiveness. And states which did not recognize this found the economies over which they presided in relative decline.

There was an 'opening up' to international investment and the world market of partial state capitalisms as varied as Argentina and Brazil, Spain and Ireland, South Korea and Egypt. And the internal economies of the established Western capitalisms were increasingly 'restructured' in accordance with a changing world division of labour.

These changes meant that the state began to lose its ability to suppress symptoms of crisis, to stop overaccumulation of capital (the 'crisis of underproduction') giving rise to a crisis of overproduction. Hence the generalized recessions of the mid-1970s and early 1980s.[138] Hence the sudden discovery by numerous Western and Third World states that the old 'Keynesian' methods or 'import substitutionist development strategies' could no longer work.

The same considerations were increasingly affecting the Eastern states as well. The old response to the bottlenecks and inflationary pressures arising from 'overinvestment' had been to shift resources from 'non-priority' to 'priority' sectors of the economy. But declining growth rates, on the one hand, and the increasing proportion of output dependent on international trade on the other, reduced enormously the resources that could be moved in this way. The strain on resources prevented many enterprises in 'priority' and 'non-priority' sectors attaining old output levels, let alone the new ones specified in the 'plans.' The economy as a whole stagnated, or even began to decline, while shortages of consumer goods and even some producer goods proliferated. The state capitalist command economy had entered a period of generalized crisis.

For a time those who ran the state tried to ward off the growing crisis through 'reforms' ('acceleration', then *Perestroika*, then a gradual introduction of market mechanisms). But reforms simply could not work and the whole of society drifted to social and political as well as economic crisis. At this point a section of the ruling class came to believe they had no choice but to allow the crisis to run its course, to allow enterprises to compete directly with each other for resources which were in short supply, even though this could only lead to the internal economy going into recession on a scale not experienced by the advanced Western countries since the 1930s.

Such a recession represents the transformation of an economy of shortages, of 'underproduction', into an economy of overproduction. That is why factories in Poland are shutting down because they cannot sell their output, and why foodstuffs are piling up in the countryside while growing numbers of people go hungry. Whether Mandel understands it or not, the dialectic of state capitalist development transformed the nearly empty Warsaw shops of 1989 into the Warsaw shops of 1990, overfull of goods that working people could not afford to buy.

It is similar shock treatment that Gorbachev says he intends to apply, under the Shatalin programme, to the USSR. I have argued at length in previous articles that the road of the market and recession will not solve the problems of the bureaucracy, and that, as in the West, the attempt to follow this path will be accompanied by continuing splits inside the ruling class.[139] The point here, however, is that significant sections of the ruling bureaucracies have felt driven in this direction by the dynamic of the command economy itself. It is a pity that people like Mandel are so blinded by inadequate theoretical formulations that they refuse to recognize this.

Two traditions on theory and practice

Towards the end of his attack on me Mandel suggests that the only reason the British SWP is interested in such arguments is because we are 'scholastic', 'hopeless splitters', only interested in 'stirring up artificial distinctions with every other revolutionary current.' But, as Lenin used to put it, 'without a revolutionary theory there can be no revolutionary practice.' And a theory which is based on contradictions and falsities cannot lead to consistent – and therefore revolutionary – practice, however subjectively revolutionary its adherents.

Theory is not some abstraction, divorced from practice. It determines how you understand a rapidly changing reality and your tasks in relation to it. At key points in history your theoretical understanding determines on which side of the barricades you find yourself. So it was that those who had a correct understanding of imperialism in the years 1914–18 had no difficulty coming out against the war, while those who simply stuck to old formulae from Marx and Engels often succumbed to the pressures to back their own ruling classes. So it was that in 1917 those old Bolsheviks who stuck to the formula of 'the democratic dictatorship of the proletariat and the peasantry' were often led to support the provisional government.

We are witnessing enormous changes in the USSR and Eastern Europe today. We cannot come to terms with such changes simply by relying on common sense formulations. As Gramsci used to insist, to base yourself on common sense is simply to accept in an uncritical manner the prevailing ideas, the ideas of the ruling class.

For 60 years rulers East and West had a common interest in claiming that Stalinism was a version of socialism, indeed, as 'actually existing socialism' the only non-utopian version. This enabled the state capitalist rulers of the East to conceal their real purposes from their own peoples and from the most militant opponents of capitalism in the West. And it enabled the rulers of the West to weaken opposition to themselves by pointing to the East and claiming that socialism entailed loss of freedom for the mass of workers. Pushed alike by both sets of rulers, it is hardly surprising that the notion entered in the 'common sense' of the great majority of the world's people.

The task of Marxist theory is to challenge such common sense. Unfortunately, instead of doing so, Mandel resorts to it in order to back up his own assertions, as when he argues that 'literally no one in these countries, or in the world, denies the evidence ... [of] a restoration of capitalism in several East European countries.'

If we are to accept ideas because of their popularity, we might as well also concede that nationalization under capitalism is a form of socialism, that Labour parties always form 'socialist' governments, and, today, that the crisis of the East European economies proves the 'failure of socialism.' All those ideas have been held as widely as the view that Eastern Europe is moving from 'socialism' to 'capitalism.'

We have to reject all these ideas because a scientific understanding of society means starting from the relations of production and exploitation – and these are not changed simply by a change in the party which runs the government, by the state taking over the means of production ... or by the state giving up some of that ownership.

If you do not challenge such 'common sense' you cannot put forward a clear, independent working class politics. For a workers' state, however deformed or degenerate, to become a capitalist state must be a step back historically, a stage in a counter-revolutionary process which Marxists should oppose. But if this is so, should Marxists not be supporting those sections of the *nomenklatura* most resistant to such a change – supporting Ligachev when he argues against privatisation, supporting the Stalin-lover Nina Andreyeva when she denounces Gorbachev's 'restorationist' tendencies, supporting Iliescu when he crushes the Bucharest students? Should Marxists perhaps have supported Honecker's efforts to use force against a movement which so easily fell under West German hegemony?

Mandel argues that no section of the Fourth International has ever fallen into such a trap. But it has in the past created illusions in those who ran the East European states. Whatever his claims today, in 1956 Mandel did encourage the belief, widespread on the reformist left East and West, that the accession of Gomulka to power guaranteed 'socialist democracy.' He did write:

The power of the movement has become irresistible. Socialist democracy will still have many battles to win in Poland. But the principal battle, that which has permitted millions of workers to identify themselves again with the workers' states, is already won.[140]

He did praise the 'new leadership' of Polish Stalinism for keeping at the head of the movement, while complaining that the reformers inside the Hungarian party leadership had not been able to do so:

> *The subtle interaction between the objective and subjective factors, between pressure from below and the crystallization of an opposition at the top of the Communist Party, an interaction which made possible the Polish victory, was missing in Hungary.*

He did go beyond mourning the Hungarian premier Imre Nagy as a victim of Khrushchev to praising him for his 'attempt to conquer the leadership of ... the revolution.'[141]

The theory of the Eastern states which Mandel adheres to has allowed many people – including some with years of activity within the Fourth International – to go much further. Isaac Deutscher did support the crushing of the East German and Hungarian risings, and so did splinter groups from the Fourth International like those led by Cochrane in the US and Lawrence in Britain. The *Militant* group in Britain (for a number of years the official section of Mandel's International) did argue that Marxists should be prepared for 'tactical' alliances with Honecker in Germany and 'sections of the *securitate*' in Romania, and did support the crushing of the Bucharest students. And the American Socialist Workers Party did not change its politics of Castro worship when, a couple of years back, it ended its 25-year-old term as one of the biggest sections of Mandel's International and insisted it was no longer 'Trotskyist.'

Slipshod theoretical formulations do not inevitably lead to reactionary practical conclusions. But they make it easier to draw them. And Mandel's formulations are slipshod. He claims that in 'Hungary, Poland and the German Democratic Republic ... a significant section of the *nomenklatura*' has 'been seen to tiptoe away from the stage of society.' But, any objective analysis of what has happened in these countries points to something else.

There has been a change of the ruling party. But it has left virtually untouched those who organize and benefit from exploitation in the enterprises, the ruling class. Not only does at least 80 per cent of industry remain in the hands of state appointees in Hungary and Poland at the time of writing, but most of the 20 per cent or so which has been privatised has passed into the ownership of those with *nomenklatura* backgrounds. The hierarchies of control in the armed forces, the police and much of the media remain in very much the same hands as before. The individuals who hold ministerial portfolios might have changed, but the key structures of the state have not.

Things are more complicated in the case of what used to be East Germany. But it is former *nomenklatura* managers who are negotiating the joint agreements between East German and Western capital. Even when there are complete takeovers from the West, many senior managers from the *nomenklatura* remain at their posts as subordinate members of the newly unified ruling class. The East German section of the main German capitalist party, the Christian Democrats, is a former front party for the *nomenklatura*, full of figures who prospered in the old East German state. And West German capitalism has found a role for sections of the old East German officer corps and even many former members of the Stasi.[142]

If, as Mandel claims, a 'restoration of capitalism' is occurring in Eastern Europe, he ought to be able to say when the decisive change, the counter-revolution, from a state representing one mode of production to one representing another, occurred. Was it with the changes of the autumn and winter of 1989? Was it with the formation of non-Stalinist governments? Was it with the privatisation of less than 20 per cent of industry? Or is it still to happen?

He hints that privatisation is the key question for instance, when he says that privatisation could lead to recession in the USSR. But in that case with only 20 per cent of the economy privately owned Poland must still have the economy of a workers' state (a workers' state with a bourgeois government?). But that economy is already experiencing a recession worse than any experienced in the West since the 1930s.

The logic of Mandel's argument is to say that the key struggle for workers is to defend what remains of the 'workers' state'

– the nationalized form of property and the old mechanisms of the command economy. It is a logic which can be very dangerous for the genuine left in the Eastern countries.

Workers are only too aware that it is the old command economy that has led to the queues, the shortages, the ecological disasters, the rising unemployment and now the recession. They hate that section of the *nomenklatura* which identifies with the old methods. That is why in the USSR the new workers' organizations have been bitterly opposed to Ryzhkov and have easily succumbed to illusions in Yeltsin with his calls for rapid privatisation. That is why in Poland Walesa can build a populist campaign for the presidency based on demagogy against the *nomenklatura* and, again, the demand for more rapid privatisation. That is why workers in East Germany fell into the trap of believing their future would best be protected by rapid incorporation into West Germany.

Genuine socialists have to warn workers that the market and privatisation offer no solution to the crisis. But we cannot do so if we give the impression that the alternative is to stick with the old ways, that somehow if the old ways had been left intact everything would be all right. Even worse is for socialists to call upon workers to make 'sacrifices' to protect the old ways.

Yet this is exactly what happened with the majority of the United Left in East Germany in the late spring of 1989. The Christian Democrats had won the general election through West German Chancellor Kohl's promise of a one-to-one exchange rate between East and West German marks. He then tried to renege on this promise, and a huge protest demonstration of workers took place. The majority of the United Left opposed this demonstration, claiming that the most important thing was to protect the nationalized East German enterprises against international competition, and that this would be more difficult with an exchange rate that gave East German workers higher rather than lower wages.

Fortunately, a minority of United Left members rejected this position, arguing that the central question was of independent organization of workers in defence of their own interests, both against their old bosses and against those West

German interests who wanted to join with the old bosses in exploiting them.[143]

Such issues will arise again and again in the Eastern states. Some sections of the bureaucracy will try to mobilize workers behind their own programme of 'reforms' and the market. Other sections will claim their defence of the old system is a defence of workers' interests. Genuine socialists have to stand firm against both sections, insisting that both want workers to pay for their crisis. But we can only do so if we are clear that the move from the command economy to the market is neither a step forward nor a step backwards, but a step sideways, from one way of organizing capitalist exploitation to another.

The importance of these arguments can be seen if you look at the history of restructuring and privatisation in countries like Britain. The biggest attacks on working class conditions and jobs usually occurred while firms remained in state ownership. Managements urged workers to accept these measures as the price of maintaining nationalization, and, in key cases like British Leyland (now renamed Rover) and British shipbuilding, won support of union leaders and senior shop stewards to this position. Then after five or ten years of repeated closures, redundancies and speed up, those same managements endorsed privatisation and increased their own salaries enormously. Privatisation came *after* the biggest attacks on workers, not before it. And union officials and stewards who saw privatisation as *the* issue, as more important than the attacks, made it more difficult for workers to fight back. We can only hope that Mandel's arguments do not lead some his followers in the East to play a similar role today.

But it is not only in the Eastern states that an understanding of state capitalism is important. The crisis of the Eastern states has led, inevitably, to a world-wide crisis among those sections of the left who used to be influenced by Stalinism. Vast numbers of people who used to believe that the Stalinist model was *the* alternative to the ruling classes of the West and the Third World are now wondering whether there is an alternative at all.

It has been this, for instance, which has allowed the leadership of the South African Communist Party – probably the only one in the world still to be growing – to justify its embrace of the mixed economy and foreign investment.[144] It is this which provided the leadership of the Greek Communist Party with its rationale for moving in two short years from Stalinism via an accommodation of Eurocommunism to the formation of a coalition government with the right-wing New Democracy party.

It is certainly not sectarian for South African or Greek revolutionaries to try to provide a clear explanation of what is happening in the Eastern states. But they cannot provide such explanations unless they argue out the issue among themselves, without any fudging. Yet Mandel is calling for such fudging when he implies it makes no difference to revolutionaries in Eastern Europe whether they accept our views or his, and calls for them all to affiliate to his International. If he were really confident in his assertion that a counter-revolution is taking place, then he would surely be insistent that those of us who do not agree should be in a different organization.

The argument over state capitalism has implications that go beyond the question of the Eastern states. In the Third World there are many regimes which have copied totalitarian features from the old Stalinist states. A state capitalist analysis enables socialists to understand where such features come from – and also to understand that they will eventually be blasted apart by the combined impact of economic crisis and a growing working class.

By contrast, without such an analysis, it is all too easy to fall into the trap of seeing these regimes as uniquely horrific, as worse than any conceivable alternative. There was such confusion in relation to Iran in the late 1980s – at the very time that the US was engaged in a massive military effort aimed at ensuring the defeat of Iran in the first Gulf War. Typical was an article by Val Moghadam which appeared in *New Left Review*:

> *How could it be seriously argued that the Islamic regime's economic policies – some populist, some statist, some anachronistic (e.g., on the ban on loan interest) – reflected 'capitalist laws of accumulation'? ... It was quite simply not a capitalist, still less a bourgeois government ... The fundamental problem was not that the regime was capitalist, but*

that it was incapable of organizing a viable and just political economy based upon democratic rights and the socio-economic needs of the population ... This was despite the fact that in the summer of 1979, the government began nationalizing all major industries, banks, insurance companies and foreign trade.[145]

So the lack of an understanding of the forms capitalism has taken in the 20th century led to the view that a Third World regime like Khomeini's was qualitatively worse than a 'normal' bourgeois regime. This was the conclusion which Fred Halliday drew in the same issue of *New Left Review*, contrasting the 'progressive position' of the 'liberal bourgeoisie' to 'the reactionary ideas and policies of Khomeini.'[146] Such analyses led to a refusal to oppose the US offensive against Iran.

Halliday had argued for years that the Eastern states were different from and superior to the West. In an article that appeared early in 1990 he still spoke of 'the degree to which there did exist in the 'communist' states a system based on different social and economic criteria' to capitalism and of 'the internationalist commitments that were one of the brighter sides of the Brezhnevite era.'[147] He went on to describe what was happening in the Eastern states as involving 'recidivism of epochal proportions.'[148] Yet without any analysis to explain these changes, he could only conclude that they undermined much of the classical Marxist analysis:

> *The greatest mistake of Marxist and socialist thinking ... was the underestimation of capitalism itself, both in terms of its potential for continued expansion and in terms of its not having within it a catastrophist teleology ...* [149]

What this necessitates, and provides the opportunity for, is a reassessment and realignment not only of Marxism and the socialist movement but the whole radical and revolutionary traditions within Western society as a whole.

Central to this he argued was a return to the liberal values of the Enlightenment, a 'recognition of how relevant pre-Marxist radical currents may be, especially in the face of the resurgent challenges of the time, clericalism, nationalism and irrationalism.'[150]

What this meant in practice for Halliday was shown in the late summer of 1990 when, in radio interviews, he urged Western military intervention against Iraq, he maintained, 'I would not think that at a future juncture, if sanctions fail, that military action to oust Iraq from Kuwait would be unjustified.'[151]

The only way the genuine left internationally can deal with such disorientation is by subjecting all the old, common sense accounts of the Eastern states to the most stringent scientific scrutiny. For this reason, we make no apology for trying to build an international tendency based on our analysis of the world system, an analysis in which the notion of state capitalism is central.

But the national organizations that make up the tendency certainly do not simply talk about state capitalism, in the way that Mandel claims. If that were true, we in Britain would never have gained the 'roots in the working class' to which Mandel refers, OSE would never have become the biggest group on the Greek far left and been able to intervene in the recent general strike and the German *Sozialistische Abeitergruppe* would never have been able to win members within the United Left in the former DDR.

Even where the organizations in our tendency are small, their work is not characterized by any abstract and sectarian fixation around the question of state capitalism. The French group, *Socialisme International*, has centred most of its activity in recent years around the demand that the left moves seriously to confront the Nazis of the *Front National* – a task which the biggest revolutionary organization in France, *Lutte Ouvrière*, refuses to consider and which the second biggest organization, the *Ligue Communiste Révolutionaire*, only began to take seriously in the early summer of 1990. *Socialisme International*'s most 'notorious' intervention on the political scene so far was in 1989 when it alone of the revolutionary organizations took an uncompromising stand on the right of girls from immigrant families to wear the Islamic veil to school in the face of a campaign against them orchestrated by the racist right.

Groups like those in the United States, Ireland, Australia, Canada, Denmark, Holland, Norway, are active in all sorts of struggles – from the defence of abortion rights to picket lines against union busting and opposition to racism and imperialism – while attempting to make revolutionary politics relevant to a new generation of activists through papers which combine theory and practice, propaganda and agitation. And all of our groups can boast an exemplary record in opposing Western war drives in the Middle East, both against Iran in the 1986 and 1987 and against Iraq more recently.

Mandel complains that our tendency is small. So is his International: we have about 6,000 supporters internationally, and his International claimed 10,000 members in 1985[152] and since then it has lost its once powerful American section, the US Socialist Workers Party. So we both count our supporters in thousands, while the world working class is about a 1,000 million strong. Neither of us should be ashamed of the fact. For two generations Stalinism dominated and disillusioned the left internationally, marginalising its opponents when it did not murder them. The question is how to build now that Stalinism itself has collapsed.

Mandel believes a small organization can become a bigger one if it fudges its analysis and avoids coming to terms with what is really happening in the world. We do not. Those of us with clear answers to the crisis of Stalinism can grow and play a positive role in the class struggle East and West. Those without such clarity may attract confused people around them for a period, but will just as surely lose them.

The impasse of schematic dogmatism

Ernest Mandel

The attempted neo-Stalinist coup in the USSR, and its dramatic aftermath, show we are entering a turning point in world history. The political tendency I belong to, the Fourth International, in common with the British SWP, condemned the coup from the start and applauded the mass workers mobilizations which contributed decisively to its defeat. But now, as has been clear for a long time, the issue is posed whether capitalism will be restored in Eastern Europe, the Soviet Union, Cuba, and China.

For us, contrary to the logic of Chris Harman and the SWP, such an outcome would signify a major victory for world imperialism. Capitalism can only be restored by inflicting major defeats on the working class. The bureaucracy in the deformed and degenerated workers states is incapable of resisting capitalist restoration; indeed, whole sections of the bureaucracy are preparing to find themselves a new niche as capitalists or in the state apparatus of a reconstituted capitalist system.

For us, the working class and the small minority of socialists in these states have to pursue a *double* struggle. First, they have to fight against the bureaucracy to the end, ensuring its political defeat. While in some circumstances it may be possible to address, and to win over, sections of the base of the old Stalinist and neo-Stalinist parties, that is not the political heart of the matter. Politically, there must be a relentless struggle to defeat the old Stalinist and neo-Stalinist parties and build mass independent unions and new workers parties.

But at the same time, socialists must resist every attempt to destroy the collectivized property relations – concretely this means battling without reservation *against* attempts to privatize enterprises and destroy the social gains of the working class – the inefficient, unfair, chronically disorganized, but nonetheless real gains of huge subsidies on rents and food, ultra-cheap housing and transport, free childcare and healthcare – and above all guaranteed employment. However disorganized and dilapidated these gains, imperialism demands their destruction to introduce full market relations; this has been a central demand as a precondition for economic aid to Hungary and Poland through the PHARE programme for example. The consequences of the integration of the GDR into West Germany has been a sharp attack on these gains – unemployment at about 40 per cent, the abolition of free childcare forcing women back into the home, rocketing rents, and prices.

We have no nostalgia for Stalinism whatever. But every revolution engenders the danger of counter-revolution. Who could believe that the re-establishment of capitalism in the USSR, China or Cuba could be anything other than a defeat? But for Chris Harman and the SWP, this is not the case. For them, this would merely be a 'step sideways' – as Chris Harman (illogically) puts it from 'state capitalism' to 'multinational(!) state capitalism' (on this unique concept see Harman's article in *International Socialism* no.46). The theory of state capitalism is incapable of responding to the needs of the dual struggle against Stalinism and capitalist restoration because of the dogma of state capitalism and the fallacious theories of the development of modem capitalism devised by the SWP to justify it.

According to the SWP, developing the theories of Hilferding and Bukharin, all modern capitalism is one or other type of 'state capitalism', with capital increasingly fused with the state. This, in the epoch of the multinational corporation, we emphatically deny. The functionality of this theoretical operation for state cap theorists is obvious; if all capitalism is some kind of state capitalism, then the fundamental differences between non-capitalist and capitalist economies can be glossed over. In order to unravel this, we shall have to go back to a discussion about what Marx thought was specific about capitalism and examine the reality of contemporary capitalism and its periodic crises.

Let us proceed then to an analysis of the SWP's mystifications about contemporary capitalism, after which we return in more detail to the political consequences of their theories.

The simplistic Marx and the logical Harman

Because we see in contemporary capitalism the living proof of Marx's theories, Harman calls us 'simplistic in the extreme.' This is a grave charge which just happens to be wrong.

Harman's overall case is that the crises in the USSR can be considered a variety of *capitalist* crisis. This involves a series of far-fetched propositions about the character of modem capitalism, and in particular the integration of capital with the state. As we shall see, this overestimation of the integration of capital with the state consistently led the Cliff-Harman school to overstate planning within contemporary capitalism, and thus to *underestimate* the possibilities of capitalist crisis.

Harman tries to deal with 'modern Western capitalism.' But that is an abstraction. There is an international capitalist economy, which is an organic (and contradictory) unity of imperialist and third world countries. As Lenin explained to Bukharin,[153] the ancestor, together with Hilferding, of Cliff's economic theories, you cannot detach the functioning of imperialism from the general laws of the capitalist mode of production, as laid bare by the three volumes of *Capital*.

Capitalism cannot exist without money capital being the starting point and the end result of production for profit. Capitalism cannot exist without generalized commodity production, without the private and not immediately social character of labour, without the contradiction between use value and exchange value inherent in the commodity.

This is indeed Karl Marx's 'oversimplification' throughout the three volumes of *Capital*, the *Grundrisse* and the manuscripts of 1861-62. You cannot consider 'capitalist' any economic system in which these laws would not be valid anymore, in which 'the state' (why not 'the party', the general secretary, or any infallible Pope?) could somehow eliminate objective laws from functioning behind the backs of people.

Everybody has the right to consider themselves as revolutionary socialists while thinking that Marx's *Capital* is 'outdated' (a product of the 19th century). But nobody has the right to attribute to Marx ideas which not only he didn't share but against which he polemicized for more than a quarter of a century.

Marx's *Capital* makes it crystal clear that the reproduction of capital, and therefore capital accumulation, and therefore economic growth under capitalism, results from the *unity of a process of value (surplus value) production and of value (surplus value) realization*. Produced but unsold commodities do not lead to capital accumulation. 'Say's Law' is nonsense. Under commodity production, output does not automatically create the demand for its own realization. That's why crises of overproduction are inevitable under capitalism.

This is true in the 20th century as it was true in the 19th century. It will be true in the 21st century too, if capitalism survives till then. If an economy emerges in which this isn't true anymore, then there would only be two possible conclusions: either that Marx's analysis of capitalism has been proven wrong, or that another economy than capitalism has emerged.

For the very same reason, as Marx precisely states in the *Grundrisse*:

> *As value constitutes the basis of capital, and as it necessarily can exist only through exchange against all equivalent [counter-value, Gegenwert is the term used by Marx], it necessarily 'repulses itself from itself.' A universal capital, without alien capitals which it confronts and with which it exchanges [not with whom it conducts 'military competition' but with whom it exchanges E.M] is therefore an impossibility.*[154]

Harman could object that he doesn't call Marx over-simplistic but only Mandel. After all, Mandel isn't Marx. Of course, he isn't, he doesn't believe to be. But the objection would only make sense if Harman could prove that Mandel did not summarize correctly the central theses of Marx's *Capital*.

He can't. We did challenge Cliff and Harman before on this. We challenge them again. No explanation is going to be offered because it just can't be offered.

In a complete reversal of Harman's position, Alex Callinicos accuses us of eclecticism and pragmatism instead of 'over-simplification.'[155] As he sees it, our rejection of monocausal explanations of economic booms and crises is incompatible with Marxism's aspiration to be a 'theory of the social totality.' Unfortunately, our rejection of monocausality is again a literal reference of Marx who wrote about the causes of economic crises:

> 'The world trade crises must be regarded as the real concentration and forcible adjustment of all the contradictions of bourgeois economy. The individual factors which are condensed in these crises must therefore emerge and must be described in each sphere of the bourgeois economy, and the further we advance in our examination of the latter, the more aspects of this conflict must be traced on the one hand, and on the other hand, it must be shown that its more abstract forms are recurring and are contained in the more concrete forms.'[156]

This is a far cry from any monocausal explanation of capitalist crises indeed.

Callinicos, harking back to Popper, contends that our way of explaining social developments through the dialectical interaction of the concrete and the abstract, the objective and the subjective, the general and the particular, the logical and the historical – which is but the reproduction of Marx's own dialectical method – 'preserves its integrity at the price of the loss of any explanatory power.'[157] Really? He then cites as proof of that 'failure', what we consider as one of our main explanatory achievements: our prediction, in the midst of the post-war boom, i.e., in the mid-1960s, that a new 'long depressive wave' would start at the end of that decade, or at the beginning of the seventies, with much more severe recessions, a much lower average rate of growth and a constantly growing permanent unemployment. Isn't that what actually did occur?

It shouldn't have occurred, it couldn't have occurred, according to the Gospel of Saint Cliff. But it did occur.

So, the shoe sits exactly on the other foot. It is the dogma of state capitalism which had no explanatory power. In order to prove the opposite, you have to go into sterile quote-culling, not looking for the real logic of ideas. It is unworthy of Alex Callinicos that he resorts to this kind of argument.

So we call upon all Marxists in and around the SWP to share our deadly sin: to prefer the sophisticated and painstaking Marx of the thousands of pages of the three volumes of *Capital*, the *Grundrisse*, and the *Manuscripts of 1861-62*, to the 'logical' simplifiers and dogmatists of the Cliff-Harman-Callinicos school. Even if we shall burn at the stake, we shall still be shouting: *eppur si muove*. Experience shows us to be right.

Or course our (Marx's) thesis (hypothesis) is really scientific because it could (can) be perfectly falsified. If there had been no crises of overproduction for half a century of a century; if there had been no serious unemployment in any imperialist country; nor any rising misery in third world capitalist countries again for half a century or a century; nor any serious 'new poverty' in the West, then the conclusion would be obvious: Marx and his minor disciples like Mandel would have been shown to be wrong. But is that the real trend of events of the last 20 years?

Fifty years behind reality

Harman insists on the fact that 'once capitalism enters its monopoly imperialist stage, it is dominated by gigantic concerns which certainly do not organize the processes of production inside them on the basis of exchange of commodities at market prices, but by a planned interaction of inputs and outputs.'

As a matter of fact, this is not only true for the 'gigantic' concerns of the imperialist stage. It was already true for any multi-divisional factory of the 19th century, e.g., steam engines or textile-machines building plants.

But what happens when the products of these concerns leave the factory? Have they to be *sold,* or can they be distributed through a 'planned interaction of inputs and outputs'? Unfortunately for Messrs, owners and managers of Ford, Phillips and De Beers, unsold cars, television sets and diamonds sold at steeply declining prices, mean less profit and less capital accumulation, in the stage of monopoly capitalism as in the stage of 'laissez-faire' capitalism.

Outside the factory, the law of value rules. And that rule reacts upon the international organization of the factory too. Monopolies try to control markets (what they really succeed in achieving is avoiding permanent cut-throat price competition). But they cannot eliminate the basic contradiction between growing objective socialization of labour and private appropriation. You cannot overcome that contradiction within the boundaries of capitalism.

Let us grant (tongue in cheek) that, during a given stage, roughly 1890-1940, 'state monopolist trusts', to take Bukharin's formula, were actually the predominant forms of capitalist firms, and that during that period, the struggle between them on the world market 'is decided in the first place by the relation between their military forces.' But Harman does not seem to have noticed that these descriptions do correspond less and less to the capitalist reality since the end of the Second World War, i.e., since nearly half a century. The main new feature of 'late capitalism' is the growing internationalization of the productive forces and, in function of that, the growing internationalization of capital itself.

But simultaneously, no 'international state' not to speak of a 'world state' has emerged. The main organizational form of capital today is not the 'state monopolist trust' but the multinational corporation, more and more independent of all states. Less than 700 of them dominate the world market. Competition between them is not decided in the first place by the 'relation between their military forces.' Otherwise, one wouldn't understand why American-based multinationals have steadily lost weight compared to Japanese and West German ones, why in other words US imperialism steadily lost its technological, industrial and financial advance compared to its competitors, while fully maintaining its military hegemony.

Of course, there is a complex concrete interaction between technological, industrial, commercial, financial, monetary, political, and military competition. This has to be examined and re-examined during each specific sub-period (business cycle period, class struggle period) of the last 40-50 years. But it remains a fact that Harman's 'updating' contemporary capitalism is nearly half a century behind objective reality.

The dogma of 'state capitalism' just does not correspond to the reality of international capitalism today. Its four main features, the multinational corporation, the continuous over-exploitation of the 'third world', the stepped-up tempo of technological innovation during the 'third technological revolution', and permanent inflation, were not taken into account by that theory. Divorce from reality in the name of defending the dogma is nearly complete.

The international capitalist economy floated towards prosperity on a sea of debt. The worldwide dollar debt alone is now estimated at $10 trillion. Germany's public debt is growing at thrice the pace of GNP. Every working day, currency speculation alone has a turnover equal to the annual volume of world trade. Yet Harman's article deals with modem capitalism without dealing with inflation, without dealing with debt, without even dealing with money.

We pointed out that the theory of state capitalism made its adepts unable to foresee the recurrent crises of overproduction, which have occurred since the early 1970s, while we were able to predict them. Harman makes an embarrassed attempt to explain them away by saying that there were no real crises of overproduction but crises of stagnation (stop-go phenomena, as the British ideology has it). This just isn't true.

There were real declines of industrial output and sales during the 1973-74 and the 1980-82 recessions. There is a real decline of output and of sales during the present recession – incidentally in Britain more than in other industrial countries. Sticking at all costs to dogma becomes an impediment for seeing and understanding reality, even when facts stare you in the face.

Today in Britain, you have a decline in industrial output of 6 per cent, three million unemployed going towards 3.5 million, and thousands of small businesses going bankrupt. Yet Harman tells these millions of victims that this is no 'real' economic crisis of overproduction, but only 'stagnation.' The unemployed and bankrupt will greet this good news with great joy, you can bet on it!

The specific nature of the Soviet economy

We pointed out the best proof that the Soviet economy is not capitalist: for more than 70 years, it hasn't experienced a general crisis of overproduction. There is a specific systemic crisis in the USSR, but is should be understood as a combined crisis of disproportionate allocation of resources and of underproduction of use-values, especially of consumer goods. We summarized our argument by saying that you cannot explain empty shops to be just a variant of (over) full shops, under-production of use-values as a variant of overproduction of commodities.

Chris Harman answers: what we have in the USSR is excess demand, which is just a phase of the capitalist business cycle. Of all Harman's arguments, this is certainly the most bizarre one. You might as well say that in the 19th century peasants in Tsarist Russia or in China were periodically hit by famine, or African peasants didn't have shoes, because of 'excess demand.' Harman does not seem to know that there is such a historical phenomenon as a chronic lack of supply (too low a level of output). He himself points out that this is precisely the case with agricultural consumer goods in the USSR since Stalin's disastrous forced collectivization policy, i.e., for a period of sixty years. So where is the 'logic'? What has 'excess demand' to do with this lack of food supply? And how does 'capitalism' (be it 'state capitalism') fit in here?

Can you imagine a situation in capitalist Britain in which for sixty years there is 'inadequate supply' compared with 'excess demand' for, say, meat, certain varieties of bread, oranges and bananas, children's shoes, well-cut women's dresses and men's suits, colour television sets which do not break down and private cars – without any capitalist doing anything about this, thereby forgoing huge immediate profits, either through manufacturing these commodities or through importing them?

Why would all the capitalists behave in such a stupid manner? Aren't they interested in maximizing profits on a short or medium-term basis, never mind the long-term consequences? Are they perhaps motivated by a fanatical addiction to 'general economic equilibrium', the *'Generalkartell'* or to the Hilferding-Bukharin-Cliff theories, rather than by the desire to maximize profits and thus increase their wealth, which is the concrete way in which capital is accumulated, again never mind the macro-economic ultimate consequences of that behaviour?

Aren't they forced to try to maximize profits for fear of going bankrupt, while no such fear existed in the USSR? Have you ever known real capitalists in the real world behaving in such an absurd way? Isn't the fact that the Soviet bureaucrats behave differently, are differently motivated, and operate in a different institutional framework, the reason why output in the USSR was not adapted to demand in these fields for six decades? Isn't that proof that the bureaucracy is not a capitalist class? This is so obvious and so elementary that one really feels embarrassed to have to point it out to intelligent Marxists like Cliff and Harman.

Comrade Harman conducts a merciless war against common sense. He has got a point. In the extremely complex world in which we are living, common sense is certainly not enough to understand what is really going on. But one thing is to say that it isn't enough. Quite another thing is to believe that it is useless. We give comrade Harman a piece of friendly advice; he should acquire a little bit of common sense. He'll be more realistic and happier with it.

According to common sense, consistent and lasting – sixty years! – underproduction of use value, is structurally different from regularly recurrent crises of overproduction of exchange values, of commodities. It wouldn't harm Harman to notice that difference.

Capitalism is generalized commodity production. This means that the law of value rules and periodically redistributes resources so as to adapt supply to demand. That is why under capitalism no 'excess demand' can exist for sixty years for whole groups of commodities (this does not imply that there cannot exist sixty years or even centuries of unsatisfied physical needs. But that again is characteristic of capitalism. Needs supported by 'demand', i.e., purchasing power, i.e., available money, are quite distinct from physical needs unsupported by money).

Under capitalism, as distinct from precapitalist commodity production, the law of value operates through the prism of the drive towards private profit maximization (private in the sense of 'for each separate firm'). Capital flows out of branches and types of activity where profits are low(er), towards branches and types of activity where profits are high(er). In each branch, firms strive to have higher profits than their competitors, above all by cutting production costs, which is the basic motor both for increasing productivity of labour – 'technical progress' – and for conducting the class struggle with the working class – for increasing the rate of exploitation.

In the Soviet economy, all these mechanisms do not function, or function only marginally. The law of value is not eliminated. But it does not rule, as little as it ruled the economy of classical China, which also had quite a lot of trade and where important amounts of money capital were being accumulated.

Contrary to what Harman alleges, the basic allocation of material and human resources in the USSR indeed occurs in the form of *a priori* allocation by the state, i.e., by the top bureaucracy, on the basis of pre-established priorities.

These priorities are determined by the desire of the bureaucracy to maintain and extend its power and privileges, not by the profit motive. In that sense, yes, again contrary to what Harman alleges, the privileges of the bureaucracy in the field of consumer goods, intrinsically linked to its monopoly of power in the state and in the factory, motivate the bureaucracy's economic behaviour. If, in the light of all the evidence revealed by *Glasnost* literature in the USSR, you continue to deny this, you again fight elementary common sense.

A fatal flaw in Cliff's chronology of the origins of the bureaucracy's power and privileges appears in that respect.

For Cliff, the function of the bureaucracy as (state capitalist) masters of the Soviet economy and hence of their consumer privileges, is supposed to be the result of stepped-up capital accumulation after 1928, under pressure of the world market, of competition with foreign capitalist powers. The real sequence of events is however different.

As Professor [Alexander] Potchekoldin, of the Institute of Marxism-Leninism revealed at the 1990 Wuppertal Bukharin Symposium, after having had access to the secret archives of the Central Committee, by 1923 a party functionary at *guberniya* level received nine times the income of an average worker. For a Central Committee functionary, it was 30 times that income. These huge income differentials were anterior to any stepped-up capital accumulation. They were anterior to any 'competition' with foreign powers. They were part of the basis of the Soviet Thermidor. And they were by and large circumscribed in the field of consumer privileges.

Indeed, thirty years ago, we pointed out the long-term disastrous consequences which would flow from the bureaucrats' basic indifference towards overall economic performance, at plant level as well as from a macro-economic point of view. In the meantime, this has become a truism in the USSR. Yet, caught in the impasse of his 'state capitalist' logic, Harman still refuses to understand this economic logic is basically different from that of capitalism.[158]

We never said that the Soviet economy is a 'waste economy' as some allege it is. We said that it *combines* economic growth with tremendous waste without a mechanism of correction of growing disproportions (a mechanism which, like Trotsky pointed out in 1932 already, could only result from a combination of socialist democracy and checks through the market).[159] Therefore, the rate of growth had to decline and the costs (losses, waste) of the system had to increase. Again, we pointed this out thirty years ago.

But the Soviet economy was not simply an economy generating 'waste.' It was also an economy characterized for a whole historical period by a higher average rate of growth than capitalism, an economy which, without being able to catch up with the USA, was indeed reducing the gap with the most advanced capitalist countries.[160] After much hemming and hawing, Harman finally recognizes this fact of life, at least, and brings us a statistic on the average rates of growth in the period 1951-75 (he could as well have taken 1928 as a starting point) quite superior to that of the average of the advanced capitalist countries. And then, by an amazing flip-flop, he tries to turn that very fact into an argument in favour of the theory of 'state capitalism'! He really has got a nerve after more than forty years of debate on that very issue in which IS-SWP defended the opposite position, including his own argument in the initial article we polemicized against.

Not content with that first flip-flop, he then adds a second one, actually underplaying the weight of the tremendous costs of bureaucratic misplanning, of the 'state (bureaucratic) command economy.' He accuses us of giving wrong information on agricultural fertilizers in the USSR as compared to the USA and Western Europe. He hasn't got the point at all.

We never said that the USSR consumes (uses) more fertilizers than the USA in the field. We said that it produces more, but that large parts of that production are not used, is not consumed, is wasted in uncovered shacks at farm level, over-filled warehouses, unloaded railways cars, etc.

All this is not the result of the functioning of the law of value. All that is not the result of socialist planning. All this is the result of arbitrary priorities in the allocation of resources by the *nomenklatura*, implying, among other things, that the part of resources devoted to the service sector and to transportation, is half or less than half of what it is in other industrialized capitalist countries.

Again, this has become a truism today in the USSR. Yet Harman sees fit to ignore it.

Harman, it is true, accepts another truism; that there are increasing bottlenecks in the Soviet economy. Generally, this truism is expressed through the formula that the Soviet bureaucracy has become unable to switch from extensive to intensive industrialization (economic growth) when the USSR's vast reserves of raw material, of relatively fertile soil, and of labour power, were drying up.

Thereby, the Soviet economy missed the boat of the third technological revolution. Its technology gap with the West was vastly growing instead of declining since the late seventies,[161] with all the consequences thereof, including in the military field. This offers the materialist explanation of Gorbachev's closer co-operation with imperialism, as against the conspiracy theory-type explanation.

But a simple question is then raised, to which Harman and Cliff cannot offer any answer. Why did this process unfold in that precise way? Why did the allegedly 'capitalist' Russian rulers not do what all the capitalists who had the means throughout the world did, and invest more in electronics, in a rather efficient way, rather than in steel, and concentrate on the most modern sectors of industry?

Why didn't they succeed in 'intensive industrialization', as even Brazil and South Korea partially did, not to speak about Japan, West Germany, France, Italy? Why did Soviet oil production, the largest in the world, become more and more inefficient, while it became more and more efficient everywhere else?

Because of a lack of capital? But under capitalism, there is never an 'absolute' shortage of capital. There is always a combination of growing flows of capital to certain branches, and growing outflows from other ones (again, that's what the rule of the law of value is all about). So why didn't these flows occur in the USSR in time and on a sufficiently large scale?

Because the Soviet workers didn't produce enough surplus value, i.e., were not exploited enough? Or because they were too much exploited? Or because there was too little food produced? Why would low agricultural output, or low real wages, prevent the production of 10 million computers, but not the production of 50 million useless tons of steel or 150,000 unused tractors?

Isn't the obvious answer that contrary to the capitalists, the Soviet bureaucrats have no vested interest in efficient output and successful competition? That it is not the profit motive which makes them tick? That conservative parasitism and not the relentless drive to increase production characterizes them?[162]

The combination between huge initial successes of Soviet planning and increasingly dysfunction of the economic system reflects the combined, double nature of Soviet society in its totality. Its achievements are the products of what still survives of the October revolution. Its failures are the results of the stranglehold of the parasitic bureaucracy on society. If Harman finds that contradictory combination illogical, that only shows that there is something wrong with his 'logic.'

In *The Revolution Betrayed*, Leon Trotsky could summarize his view of that dual contradictory nature of the Soviet economy in a way, which, fifty years before the events, reads as perfect anticipation of what has happened in the USSR since the late seventies and the early eighties:

The progressive role of the Soviet bureaucracy coincides with the period devoted to introducing into the Soviet Union the most important elements of capitalist technique. The rough work of borrowing, imitating, transplanting, and grafting, was accomplished on the basis laid down by the revolution. There was, thus far, no question of any new word in the sphere of technique, science, or art. It is possible to build gigantic factories according to a ready-made Western pattern by bureaucratic command – although to be sure, at triple the normal cost. But the further you go, the more the economy runs into the problems of quality, which slips out of the hands of a bureaucracy like a shadow. The Soviet products are as though branded with the grey label of indifference. Under a nationalized economy, quality demands a democracy of producers and consumers, freedom of criticism and initiative – conditions incompatible with a totalitarian regime of fear, lies and flattery.

Behind the question of quality stands a more complicated and grandiose problem which may be comprised in the concept of independent, technical and cultural creation (...) The socialist culture will flourish only in proportion to the dying away of the state. In that simple and unshakeable historic law is contained the death sentence of the present political regime in the Soviet Union. Soviet democracy is not the demand of an abstract policy, still less an abstract moral. It has become a life-and-death need of the country.[163]

Yet these prophetic words were developed on the basis of the theory that the Soviet Union is a bureaucratized workers state. Maybe that theory isn't so wrong after all.

Harman is making a lot of capital out of the fact that today, the growth of the Soviet economy is grinding down to stagnation and even going into negative growth. But this is a *result* of the gradual decomposition of the way that economy functioned for sixty years, not a reflection of that functioning. If a bridge is, through lack of maintenance and repair, in danger of collapsing, and traffic is therefore gradually reduced on it, that is no proof of the fact that that traffic was never dense there in yesteryear, or that the bridge served no useful purpose from the start.

In the same vein is his allegation that today's shops in Poland, which are full of commodities (exchange values) which find no customers, are the products of yesterday's empty shops. They aren't. They are the results of the decomposition of a system which, for decades, was characterized by a shortage of consumer use values, caused by insufficient and inadequate output, and to which is now substituted a system of increasing output of exchange values.

Bureaucrats and capitalists

The particular character of the behaviour of the Soviet bureaucrats, especially at the plant level, quite different from that of capitalists, can be explained by their material interests and by the basic features of the Soviet economy after the victory of the bureaucratic political counter-revolution, the Soviet Thermidor.

The power of the bureaucracy is based upon the usurpation of power from the working class, its de facto disenfranchisement and elimination from all exercise of power, in the state as well as in the economy. It also implies a severe limitation (in the first stage, even a severe restriction) of workers' consumption. Under these circumstances, only the immediate material interest of the bureaucrats could become the direct motor for the implementation of the bureaucratic plan.

To believe otherwise, to believe that people act as direct embodiments of objective social laws, including the need of capital accumulation, without the mediation of their private interests, is a naive rationalistic (in reality idealistic) illusion. Under capitalism also, the laws of capital accumulation are realized through the mediation of individual capitalists trying to further their private interests, not independently from these.

In the USSR, the realization of the plan is dependent upon the private interests of the bureaucrats in a two-fold way. Precisely because they are not private owners of the means of production, the individual bureaucrats in the first place crave for stability of tenure. The threat of losing their jobs (under Stalin: losing liberty if not life) or the possibility of career advancement is a very real one. The income of the bureaucrats is directly tied to this stability of tenure, which gives them access to many non-monetary advantages.

In addition, the money income they receive depends upon fulfilment and 'overfulfilment' of the plan. A small difference say between fulfilling the plan, realizing only 98 per cent of the foreseen target, or overfulfilling at 102 per cent, can make a difference in the bureaucrats' income of as much as 50 per cent if not more through various premiums etc.

But bureaucratic planning was characterized from the start by huge disproportions, as indicated above. These led to permanent irregularities in supply, chronic scarcities, constant interruptions in production. All these features of bureaucratic – as opposed to socialist – planning make it difficult to fulfil and overfulfil the plan.

In order to defend their material interests, the bureaucrats have recourse to a typical reaction, quite distinct from the normal behaviour of capitalists. They will systematically try to hoard reserves (of raw material, labour power, equipment) regardless of cost.[164] It is simply not true that Soviet industry is characterized by a constant overstretching of resource-use, by an extreme lack of reserves (of stocks of 'productive factors') as so many commentators allege. There are huge reserves. But they are generally scattered over a great number of production and distribution units. They are not at the disposal of the central planning authorities (of the state).

Furthermore, to be able to have these 'cushions' available, the individual bureaucrats chronically give false information to the centre. They not only hide these reserves in their reports. They will also systematically undervalue the existing productive capacity and overestimate the need for receiving additional resources. Their logic is simple. The lower the recognized production capacity of the plant, the lower the predictable plan targets, the easier these will be realized, and the higher will be their incomes and their chances of keeping their jobs and continuing their upward careers. The same applies, roughly speaking, for the requested additional resources. The higher these will be, the easier it will be to fulfil and overfulfil the plan.

But the central authorities know all that. They, therefore, start from the assumption that the information they get from the production and distribution units is partially false. Their reaction is again two-fold.

First, they send an army of controllers to the units, in order to check the data. Second, they change systematically and in a quite arbitrary way, the mass of data received from below when they formulate the plan targets. *Systematic misinformation becomes generalized.* Here you have the secret of the bureaucratized planned economy, of the hypertrophy of Department III (unproductive expenditures, a huge army of controllers-checkers-policemen of all types) and of the growing dysfunction of the economy.

Yet Harman's representation of the Soviet economy even formally denies the existence of Department III. It mixes the output of machines and raw material used for expanded reproduction, i.e., capital accumulation, i.e., economic growth, together with the output of weapons, rusting steel hoards, cotton never delivered to textile factories, luxury 'Culture Palaces' for the bureaucracy, potatoes rotting on the fields, in a single Department I. How such goods contribute, from the point of view of use values, to expanded reproduction and economic growth remains a mystery. Here the 'state capitalist' theoreticians' disregard for the basic contradictions of the commodity, the contradiction between use value and exchange value, between private labour and social labour, and of capitalism as being generalized commodity production, really comes into its own.

Contrary to the logic of socialist planning, bureaucratic planning has a built-in element of opacity, or lack of transparency, not corrected by the market and by the law of value. Paradoxically, the Soviet economy was characterized as much if not more by a lack of real planning, by semi-planning of pseudo-planning, as it was characterized by a lack of socialist democracy (workers control) and of necessary checks through the market.

One should add that the basic logic of any bureaucracy – including a capitalist one, in bourgeois society – and the basic logic of capitalism are quite different. Bureaucrats operate on the basis of an economy of *a priori* allocation of resources (*Zuteilungswirtschaft*). They, therefore, have a vested interest in spending these resources entirely, regardless of results, lest the allocation be automatically reduced for the following year. They also have a vested interest in demanding more resources, regardless of results.

Capitalists, on the contrary, get their income only *a posteriori,* when the goods they own are sold. For that reason, as well as in function of the general pressure of competition they are submitted to, they have a vested interest in cost-cutting and exact cost accounting. They are unable to operate 'regardless of cost.'

This does not mean that their economic behaviour is more 'rational' than that of the bureaucrats. What is 'rational' on a micro-economic scale, at the level of the individual firm or trust, can have extremely irrational effects from a macro-economic and macro-social point of view.[165] What is 'rational' in the short run can be extremely irrational in the long run.

We only state that the behaviour of bureaucrats and that of capitalists is basically different because they are embedded in different socio-economic frameworks and submitted to different constraints, not that the one is 'better' than the other.

The Soviet economy and the world market

Derek Howl makes a half-hearted attempt to save the relation of the 'state capitalist' theory with Marxism – i.e., the question of the function of the law of value in the Soviet economy – by stating that the Soviet bureaucracy 'compares' the production costs in Russia with those of its foreign 'competitors'[166] and in that way submits to the law of value. Unwittingly, he thereby puts his finger on a key weakness of the 'state capitalist' dogma.

A capitalist firm certainly 'compares' its production costs with those of its national and international competitors. But precisely under capitalism, 'comparison' is only the starting point of the process, and in no way its decisive aspect.

Whatever the mistakes these comparisons may contain they always involve predictions, projections, extrapolations, i.e., strong margins of error. The real test is that of realization of profit. Under capitalism, only those firms are successful in competition which have a higher than average rate of profit. And one of the key contradictions of the system is precisely the tendency of the average rate of profit to fall, not in the first place because of 'oversupply of capital', as Howl alleges, but as a result of the increase in the organic composition of capital.

Surplus-value production (valorisation of capital) is only introduced in Marx's analysis of the tendency of the rate of profit to decline as a countervailing force unable to stop the rot because, basically, the increase in surplus-value produc-tion cannot be proportional to the increase in the organic composition of capital in value terms.

But this whole central part of volume III of *Capital* isn't even mentioned by Howl. After presenting us with the mysti-fication of a capitalism without money, we now get from the SWP leadership the additional mystification of a capitalism without the tendency of the average rate of profit to decline.

But the attempt to explain 'capitalism' (be it 'state capital-ism') through relations with the world market ('comparisons with foreign competitors') has another unreal and reality-dis-torting aspect, which we already pointed out in our debate with Michael Kidron in the late 1960s.[167] The pre-revolutionary Russian economy, like the economy of the East European states (with the exception of the Bohemian part of Czechoslovakia) was an underdeveloped economy, unable to fully modernise and industrialise in the framework of the world market.[168]

'Competition' with foreign 'powers' meant in practice that these countries had a semi-colonial economic structure. They were condemned to specialize in the output and export of raw materials and agricultural products. Their modernisation was largely blocked through that dependence.

If they could break out of that dependence in Russia first, in eastern Europe later, it was precisely because they largely could free themselves from dependence upon the world market, because they despotically suspended 'competition' with 'foreign powers.' This is exactly the way in which the rule of the law of value was eliminated in these countries. For the law of value rules in the first place through the world market.[169]

The decisive test of the restoration of capitalism today would be precisely such a restoration of the rule of the law of value through the world market, i.e., large-scale reversal of these countries to a semi-colonial pattern of output, to their specialization in those sectors of production where they are relatively more competitive than in more modem industry. The future of a capitalist Poland, Hungary, Lithuania, Georgia, Ukraine, and Russia would be closer to Portugal, Greece, and Turkey than to that of Italy or Finland. The social implications would be similarly disastrous.

The acid test of practice

The SWP leaders have argued for decades that not accepting the 'state capitalist' nature of the USSR would lead socialists to wrong, if not counter-revolutionary positions in front of workers uprisings in that and similar countries. We have already shown that this prognosis hasn't been borne out by history. Harman comes back to this issue in his second article. But he introduces two red herrings.

First he alleges, against all the facts, that we somehow had illusions about the possible self-reform of the bureaucracy, and that we even preferred, at least in the case of Poland and Hungary, such self-reform ('revolution from above') to revolution from below, i.e., the overthrow of the bureaucratic dictatorship by mass action. As we said before, this is slander pure and simple. Not for one day since we started to deal with the question of the nature of the USSR in the mid-1940s, did we abandon the perspective and the fight for political revolution following Trotsky's and our movement's tradition since 1932.[170]

The quotes which Harman uses to try to insinuate that this is untrue, do not prove that at all. They just state that there is an inevitable interaction between rising mass discontent and rising mass action in these countries on the one hand, and internal divisions inside the bureaucracy on the other hand. Experience has borne that out. Nobody can deny that Rákosi, Gerő, Kádár, Nagy and Pál Maléter did not take an identical position towards the Hungarian revolution of 1956.

In fact, not only were they fighting on *different* sides of the barricades, but Gerő and Kádár had Nagy and Maléter shot. To note these facts, independently from the correctness of precise predictions in that respect, is not in any way to 'capitulate' before Stalinism, any more than noting the post-war long boom meant capitulating to Stalinism. Everything depends upon the political and practical conclusions you draw from recognizing these facts of life. The conclusions we drew from these observations about the divisions inside the bureaucracy were to continue the struggle for defending the workers' interests and the fight to political revolution.

Then Harman introduces a second red herring. Some people associated with the general approach of 'workers' statism' are alleged to have actually developed quite wrong positions. He then goes on insinuating that this is somehow the 'logical' outcome of 'workers' statism.' This is presented without any causal proof or empirical evidence. It is just demagogic mudslinging.

It is based on one of the classical sophisms of deduction: the abusive and unsubstantiated generalization of single cases. It goes as follows: 'When I disembarked in Calais, I saw a red headed woman. As this woman was French it follows that all French women are red headed.' No, it does not follow at all.

'Jacek Kuroń, as cabinet minister of a reactionary pro-capitalist government, has been responsible for mass unemployment and the reduction of the Polish workers' real wages by 35 to 50 per cent. As Jacek Kuroń has been and continues to be a resolute defender of the theory that the USSR is state capitalist, it follows that this theory leads to radical anti-working-class policies.' No, it does not follow at all.

Or better still: 'Stalin committed terrible crimes. As he referred to himself as a Marxist, it follows that Marx and Marxism throughout the world lead to terrible crimes.' No, it does not follow at all.

The use of such polemical gimmicks serves no positive purpose whatsoever for socialists and the struggle for socialism. It should be radically banned from any serious theoretical and political discussion by all responsible socialists. It is totally counter-productive. It can only discredit those who use it.

In fact, if one wants to 'infer' anything from how different revolutionary currents reacted to changes in Eastern Europe and the USSR, the inference goes in exactly the opposite direction of what Chris Harman alleges. All sections of the Fourth International, without a single exception, rejected the perspective of self-reform of the bureaucracy. All sections maintained and maintain their course towards political revolution. But all sections also maintained their analysis of the USSR and similar societies as bureaucratized workers' states, societies frozen in transition between capitalism and socialism by the bureaucratized dictatorship. So, 'workers' statism' does not 'logically' lead to any concession to the idea of possible self-reform of the bureaucracy.

We are ready to take responsibility for everything we wrote and did, and everything which the movement to which we belong wrote and did, including its mistakes, and try to correct these and discover their roots. But we don't take any responsibility for what Isaac Deutscher, who left the Trotskyist movement in 1938 and therefore never was a member of the Fourth International, did or wrote after that date, while we respect his writings and the service he has obviously rendered in rehabilitating Trotsky in the eyes of a large international audience.

And even less can we take responsibility for what Fred Halliday or Val Moghadam write or do, who have never been members of the Fourth International or even Trotskyists.

But the real issue is very important indeed: what are the practical political implications of the two different positions regarding the social nature of the USSR and similar societies on the way revolutionary socialists have to intervene in the unfolding social conflicts in these countries?

Harman cites two insignificant episodes of the alleged usefulness of the 'state capitalist' position for correct intervention in Eastern Europe. His examples are not convincing. In the concrete case of the ex-GDR, our comrades of the Revolutionary Socialist Group (in Eastern Germany) who support the position that the USSR is a bureaucratized workers state, were also in favour of supporting the mass demonstrations to which Harman refers.

The issue of privatization, which is a central issue of social and political struggles in the USSR and in several Eastern European countries is a thousand times more decisive for judging political orientation than the question of whether to participate or not in this or that particular demonstration. The SWP comrades consider that vital question as a 'side issue.' That is utterly preposterous and irresponsible.

If large-scale privatisation of big industry occurs in the USSR, there will be between 30 and 40 million unemployed. Initial privatisation has already led to the ex-GDR to the highest level of unemployment any European country has known, higher than in the 1929-33 crisis: nearly 50 per cent. Can a responsible socialist or even trade unionist be indifferent or neutral on that issue?

Dragging their feet, the SWP leaders finally say that they are also against privatisation, like they are against privatisation of nationalized industries in Britain. But this does not get them off the hook.

For as Cliff himself correctly pointed out since the Attlee government, nationalizations of certain branches of British industry were in the interests of the private sector of British capitalism, were indeed necessary to prop them up. State property in the USSR cannot be interpreted as propping up any private sector in that country. Nationalized industries in Britain did not prevent large-scale unemployment from arising precisely for that reason. Nationalized property *did* prevent large-scale unemployment in the USSR for over half a century.

Harman and Cliff are caught in the trap of their qualifying state property in the USSR as 'capitalist.' If it really is, then its suppression certainly does not make any important difference. But unfortunately for comrade Harman, it makes a tremendous difference for tens of millions of workers in the USSR and millions in Eastern Europe. It has already given rise and will give rise to massive struggles. In this fight, we are unconditionally on the side of the workers who oppose privatisation in practice, regardless with what ideology and regardless whether a section of the bureaucracy also supports them.

We do not accept the choice of the neo-liberal pro-capitalists: either privatisation or state despotism. We reject both state despotism and despotism of the market (of private wealth). We stand for a third economic model: planned democratic self-management – Trotsky called it 'producer/consumers democracy' – in which the masses decide themselves, in a democratic way, the priorities of what to produce, how to produce it and how to distribute it.

We stand for collective, social property as against private property of the great means of production and exchange. How that collective property will be organized, what could be the articulation of control of workers of each factory, of each industrial branch, of each town, of each region, of each Republic, of the Union in its totality, on the means of production and on current output, this is a question to which nobody has any definite answer, and on which the Soviet workers and revolutionary socialists will have to learn from new practice and many current debates.

Harman then raises a rhetorical question:

For a workers' state, however deformed or degenerate, to become a capitalist state must be a step back historically, a stage in a counter-revolutionary process which Marxists should oppose. But if this is so, should Marxists not be supporting those sections of the nomenklatura most resistant to such a change – supporting Ligachyov when he argues against privatisation, supporting the Stalin-lover Nina Andreyeva when she denounces Gorbachev's 'restorationist' tendencies, supporting Iliescu when he crushes the Bucharest students? Should Marxists perhaps have supported Honecker's efforts to use force against a movement which fell so easily under West German hegemony?

But this 'logic' again corresponds to a formalistic, mechanistic schema, distorting the real historical process and the real historical alternatives.

The collapse of the bureaucratic dictatorships in Eastern Europe, and the deep systemic crisis in the USSR, occur under the direct impact of huge mass mobilizations in Eastern Europe and of rising mass mobilizations in the USSR. Thereby a dynamic of political change, a pre-revolutionary dynamic, has started. This dynamic can have three different outcomes: a reconsolidation of the bureaucratic dictatorship, which would be a defeat for the working class, a political counter-revolution; a restoration of capitalism, i.e., social counter-revolution, which would be an even graver defeat for the working class; a victory of the political revolution which would mean the victory of the working class.

We are convinced that only a militant, self-active, self-organized and increasingly politically conscious working class can prevent a restoration of capitalism. We are convinced that the Ligachyovs, Honeckers, Ceaucescus, Deng Xiaopings et al are totally unable to prevent this. On the contrary: any repression of the mass movement, irrespective of its immediate effects and of its motivations, will assist the restoration of capitalism by driving the great majority of the masses politically into the pro-bourgeois camp.

Given all the disastrous political, ideological, moral consequences of the bureaucratic dictatorship on the present level of class consciousness of the Soviet working class, that class needs more time and the de facto enjoyment of democratic freedoms in order to accumulate the necessary experience in the struggle for reconquering its capacity to fight for power.

For that reason, the defence and extension of already existing democratic freedoms – never mind whether you call them *Glasnost* or not – is an absolute precondition for a successful struggle against the restoration of capitalism. Whenever these freedoms are threatened by whatever force, socialists have to oppose these threats as resolutely as they oppose privatisation, irrespective of whether any section of the bureaucracy joins in that fight, and under what ideological banners the workers defend democratic freedoms.

In other words: socialists in the USSR and Eastern Europe have to fight on two fronts: against privatisation and for democratic rights (freedoms, space of operation), regardless whether different sections of the bureaucracy join in these different struggles.

This might appear 'illogical' for formalists. But it corresponds to the immediate and historical needs of the working class, in the USSR and on a world scale.

Any radical privatisation of large factories in the USSR but also any radical suppression of de facto existing freedoms, return to a Brezhnev not to say a Stalin type dictatorship, would be a disaster for the Soviet and the international working class.

This position is completely coherent with the Fourth International's view of the historical place of the political revolution in the process of world revolution. But this we do not need to develop here.

But where is the civil war without which a victorious restoration of capitalism, a victorious social counter-revolution, would be impossible, according to Trotsky and the Fourth International, thunder Harman and Derek Howl?[171]

Trotsky and the Fourth International supporters of the theory of bureaucratized workers' states in fact never said that a civil war was *unavoidable* in order to restore capitalism in the USSR. They only said that on the road of restoration of capitalism, the resistance of the working class would have to be broken. What form that would take would obviously depend on the dimension and the political awareness of that resistance. Here is what Trotsky wrote on the subject in 1936:

If – to adopt a second hypothesis – a bourgeois party were to overthrow the ruling Soviet caste, it would find no small number of ready servants among the present bureaucrats and privileged circles in general. A purgation of the state apparatus would, of course, be necessary in this case too. But a bourgeois restoration would probably have to clean out fewer people than a revolutionary party. The chief task of the new power would be to restore private property of the means of production. First of all, it would be necessary to create conditions for the development of strong farmers from the weak collective farms, and for converting the strong collectives into producers' co-operatives of the bourgeois type – into agricultural stock companies. In the sphere of industry, denationalization would begin with the light industries and those producing food. The planning principle would be converted for the transitional period into a series of compromises between state power and individual 'corporations' – potential proprietors, that is, among the Soviet captains of industry, the emigre former proprietors and the Soviet captains of industry.[172]

This reads as a near-total description of what is going on today in Eastern Europe and what has started in the USSR. There is no mention here of civil war.

A good illustration of the differences in method

The underlying differences in method, schematic formalism and dogmatism as opposed to scientific dialectical thinking, are clearly revealed in Callinicos' critique of our analysis of World War II as 'five wars in one.'

Again trying to turn our strong points against us, Callinicos accuses us of 'syncretism' and 'scholasticism' ('the subtle skills of a medieval school man to distinguish relevant factors – for example to distinguish no less than five distinct wars within the Second World War... The effect is to deprive social theory of the interaction with potentially disconfirming observations.').[173] The last sentence is a perfect non sequitur, and a near perfect refutation of the dialectic. If you note contradictory elements of reality, you are supposed to 'deprive social theory of the interaction with potentially disconfirming(?) observations.' You are forbidden to start from the assumption that reality is contradictory and condemned to assume that really existing contradictions automatically 'disconfirm' social theory. All references made to formalistic monocausal schemas, i.e., preconceived dogmas, not to the real living world and to attempts to develop 'social theories' which take in advance into account the existence of these contradictions and try to explain them. The rejection of dialectical thought is finally based upon the rejection of the dialectical nature of objective reality itself.

In the night, all cats are grey. You can then develop monocausality into a systematic attempt to reduce 'totality' to a single colour scheme, i.e., the rejection of the colour spectrum. But like the great dialectician Goethe wrote: Eternally green is life's golden tree. In the real world's rich totality to which Marx refers – which is never monocausal or monocoloured – people are said to be colour-blind, if because of an obsession with a 'single basic principle', they only distinguish one colour, grey, or in the best of cases, two colours: black and white.

So, let us move on from schematic formalism to the 'eclectic' question of what happened in the real historical process.

Yes, World War II was predominantly an inter-imperialist war, which didn't fulfil any progressive function, which had to be condemned and opposed by all socialists. But it was not only that.

The war of the Chinese people against their attempted enslavement by Japanese imperialism was not an inter-imperialist war. It served an eminently progressive purpose. It was a just war, which had to be supported by all socialists.

Likewise, the war of the Soviet peoples against enslavement and mass slaughter by Nazi imperialism – we repeat: the *Generalplan Ost* implied the planned slaughter of 100 million Slav, Jewish, Asian *Untermenschen* – was not an inter-imperialist war. It served a highly useful purpose. It was a just war which socialists the world over, and in the first place the Soviet workers had to support 100 per cent (as Trotsky consistently called upon them to do, and as they happily did).

Likewise, the Indian, Algerian, Indonesian, Indochinese, Filipino peoples' uprisings against their imperialist overlords and butchers were not an inter-imperialist war. Again, it served a highly progressive purpose. Only lackeys of imperialism could oppose these uprisings and wars.

And finally, the uprising of the Warsaw ghetto, of the Yugoslav, Greek, Italian, Polish masses against the Nazi butchers, was not an episode of an inter-imperialist war. It was a just and legitimate revolt against mass murder and overexploitation. It was perfectly legitimate, highly useful and had to be enthusiastically supported by all socialist internationalists.

So, there you have your five wars in one. Before you crack cheap jokes about these distinctions involving the fate of a billion and a half people, please try to refute the concrete analysis. You'll have a hard time doing that. The fact that these five wars were up to a certain point enmeshed does not suppress in any way the specificity of each of them – except if you substitute schematic formalism to the concrete analysis of a concrete situation. Lenin *dixit*.

Opportunists make a pretext of the undeniably particular nature of Nazi and Japanese imperialism to arrive at the conclusion that the Indian, Indonesian, Algerian oppressed people had no right to rise against their imperialist overlords, as long as the world war was going on, lest they 'objectively' strengthen the Nazi and Japanese imperialists (which wasn't even true 'objectively'). They likewise argued that the American, British, Australian, Canadian workers had no right to defend their class interests and class independence, lest they 'objectively' help Hitler and Togo (which was slanderous nonsense).

Sectarian dogmatists, on the other hand, make a pretext of the predominantly inter-imperialist character of World War II – which is undeniable – in order to negate any relative autonomy of the peoples and mass struggles of the four other wars going on simultaneously.

'Objectively' these wars and uprisings they said, could only help one of the two imperialist camps (which again was 'objectively' totally untrue). So parallel to the opportunists they preached abstentionism, i.e., 'attentist' submission to overexploitation and mass slaughter, as long as the 'imperialist war' had not ended everywhere, presumably by instantaneous, simultaneous revolution in all countries.

The uneven, combined, and contradictory character of real mass struggles is explained away in the name of a 'unifying principle.' In practice, and in spite of all good intentions, this amounts to preaching passivity and resignation to fatality.

We believe that the duty of revolutionary socialists is exactly the opposite one: encouraging and supporting resistance, rebellion, popular uprisings and revolutions, while trying to unfold class independence and self-activity, but without transforming the acceptance of these political contents into an ultimatistic precondition for giving critical support to progressive, just, legitimate mass struggles.

Incidentally, while World War I was undoubtedly more 'homogeneous' and 'unilaterally' inter-imperialist than World War II, Lenin, who was light-years away from schematic dogmatism, perfectly recognized the seeds of 'several wars in one' even then. He wrote in July 1916, in a polemic against his fellow revolutionary internationalists Rosa Luxemburg and Herman Gorter, in a long article entitled 'Balance sheet of a discussion on the right of nations to self-determination':

> If in 1917 Belgium was annexed by Germany and it rose up in 1918 to free itself... while refusing to support the insurrection of the annexed regions, objectively we become annexers.[174]

He continues by declaring just the uprising of the Irish people against British imperialism like all uprisings in the colonies, in spite of them taking place within an imperialist war (there you have already 'embryonically' three wars in one).
And then he makes a more general point:

> To believe that the social revolution is conceivable without insurrection in the small colonial and European nations, without revolutionary explosions by a part of the petit-bourgeoisie with all its prejudices, without movement of the proletarian and semi-proletarian masses who don't

possess an anti-capitalist, an anti-clerical, anti-monarchical or anti-nationalist consciousness – is to repudiate the social revolution. It is like imagining that an army would take up a position and say 'We are in favour of imperialism', and that that would be a social revolution! It is only by starting from this pedantic and ridiculous point of view that you could abusively call the Irish insurrection a 'putsch.'

Whoever waits for a 'pure' social revolution won't live long enough to see it. They would be a revolutionary only in words, who understands nothing of what a real revolution is.[175]

Ridiculous pedantism! Revolutionary in words who does not understand a real revolution! It is not we who are saying it but Lenin, – and the attitude of the SWP comrades towards what happened during and after World War II in Yugoslavia, China, Algeria, India, Indonesia, Indochina etc, comes dangerously close to justifying Lenin's harsh judgement. There you have the two different methods of approach nicely illustrated.

Following numerous bourgeois, neo-Stalinist, Euro-communist, social democratic and sectarian critics, Alex Callinicos takes on Trotsky for his allegedly mistaken predictions about world developments in 1939. He again accuses Mandel of transforming Marxism into a theory which has lost any explanatory power[176] by trying to 'save' Trotsky's prediction through changing the life span.

But what is the truth here? In what way was Trotsky's alleged 'urgency' tied to the inner logic of his analysis about capitalist decline?

The famous sentence from 'The USSR in War' is most often only quoted partially – including now by Callinicos. It does not say that there would be a world-wide slave totalitarian society in case the war did not end in victorious revolutions. It does say: 'If, however, it is conceded that the present war will provoke not revolution [Trotsky does not say victorious revolutions E.M.] but a decline of the proletariat, then there remains another alternative'.[177]

That prediction (its 'explanatory power') has already shown

to be much less wrong than Callinicos and other critics light-mindedly alleged. After all, the war did provoke revolutions, if not in the 'pure' form the pedants think social revolutions can only occur. And the war did not provoke a decline but a new rise of the proletariat, again not in the same form as after 1916, but still a new rise, not a decline. So, the succinct formula did give us after all some 'explanatory power' to explain what actually happened from 1945 till 1949.

But what about the narrow time limit, Trotsky's alleged 'urgency'?

In the autumn of 1939 Trotsky formulated his initial thought in few words, in the midst of a faction fight and in order to deal with the central historical alternative raised by that faction fight. A few months later, he returned to the same subject in a more elaborate and thorough way, correcting any impression that the alternative had to be resolved at short notice. In his political testament, the May 1940 Manifesto of the Emergency Conference of the Fourth International, he wrote:

> There remains the question of leadership. Will not the revolution be betrayed, this time too, inasmuch as there are two Internationals in the service of imperialism while the genuine revolutionary elements constitute a tiny minority? In other words: shall we succeed in preparing in time a party capable of leading the proletarian revolution? In order to answer this question correctly, it is necessary to pose it correctly [It is as if Trotsky had foreseen critics of the Callinicos type]. Naturally, this or that uprising may end and surely will end in defeat owing to the immaturity of the revolutionary leadership. But it is not a question of a single uprising. It is a question of an entire revolutionary epoch.
>
> The capitalist world has no way out, unless a prolonged agony is so considered. It is necessary to prepare for long years, if not decades, of wars, uprisings, brief interludes of truce, new wars, and new uprisings... The question of tempos and time intervals is of enormous importance; but it alters neither the general historical perspective not the direction of our policy.[178]

Has that analysis, without any short-term urgency embodied in it, but based on the 'general historical perspective', no explanatory power for what really did happen after World War II?

Again, the shoe fits the other foot. In his obsession with 'unified theory' and 'monocausalism', Alex Callinicos does not seem to notice that at the end of World War II, we did after all have revolutions – or the beginning of revolutions – in Yugoslavia, Greece, Italy, Indochina, Indonesia, China, as well as pre-revolutionary crises in India and France.

In the fifties, we did have the Bolivian revolution, the Algerian revolution, the Hungarian revolution, the revolution in South Vietnam, the Cuban revolution. In the sixties we did have May 68 in France and its aftermath in Italy. Then we had the Portuguese revolution and the Nicaraguan revolution. And this list is by no means exhaustive.

In the meantime, we have also had 'local' wars which have already cost more deaths than the whole First World War. So, has Trotsky's analysis-prognosis proven to have been wrong?

It is true that Trotsky and the Fourth International seriously underestimated the duration of the 'brief interlude of truce' inside the imperialist countries, i.e., the long post-war boom and the impressive development of the productive forces (including the main productive force: the proletariat) which corresponded to it. We corrected that mistake a bit late, but not so late, in 1953. But Trotsky's overall analysis was certainly more correct than that of all those tendencies who said: revolution is out, full stop; or: revolution is out for a whole historical epoch, full stop; or capitalism is prosperous on a world scale... or the proletariat is historically on the decline, full stop.

Incidentally, it would be easy to prove that Trotsky and the Trotskyist movement developed the theory of at least 'four wars in one' (i.e., the progressive nature of the war of self-defence of Russia and China against imperialist aggressors and or uprisings of colonial people, as distinct from the reactionary nature of the inter-imperialist war) years before 1939-40. And before dying, Trotsky started to express himself clearly in favour of judging progressive the resistance struggles of the European peoples against Nazi occupation too. So far from being a theory developed after the facts to try to be 'right in any case', the theory of five wars in one was actually developed before the events, predicted them correctly, and created the basis of adequate socialist intervention in them.

Permanent revolution in 'third world' countries

Again: this is not a moot academic question. It raises key problems of judgement, policy, intervention, action, by revolutionary socialists.

If you have an essentially ideological approach to class struggles, mass struggles and genuine popular revolutions, i.e., revolutions with massive participation of toiling masses, then you can, of course, dismiss the Indochinese, the second Vietnamese, the Yugoslav, and especially the Chinese revolutions as being no social revolutions at all, because they were manipulated, channelled, led by Stalinists and finally resulted in bureaucratic dictatorships. If it can be proven that these uprisings are guided by 'petit-bourgeois' or 'bourgeois' ideas and (or) organizations, then they are not workers uprisings at all but bourgeois uprisings. *Ergo* the working class equals the bourgeoisie (for the state caps, the working class equals the bureaucracy in said revolutions).

For Marx social classes are objective categories, independent from the level of their self-consciousness. Roman slaves were certainly a social class, even if they had no 'slave consciousness' and were not conscious of being a class.

In bourgeois society, given the specific nature of socialist revolution, the level of class consciousness is a decisive element for determining the outcome of the class struggle. But it is not a decisive criterion for determining whether a given struggle represents a form (stage) of class struggle. And the same applies *mutatis mutandis* to the societies in transition between capitalism and socialism.

Callinicos sees a 'drift to Stalinism' in the fact that we recognized social revolutions taking place in countries like Yugoslavia, China etc, not to speak about Cuba and Nicaragua.

For him, these were only 'movements for national liberation.' He thereby joins all those – Mensheviks and Stalinists – opponents of the theory (better: the strategy) of permanent revolutions, all those advocates of a revolution by stages, who argue that it is possible to realise the central tasks of the national-democratic revolution (national independence and radical land reform) without destroying the class rule of the bourgeoisie-cum-landlords-cum-foreign capital, and without destroying the bourgeois state.

Confusing the class content of the state with the nature of its political leadership, Callinicos tries to defend the idea that the state in Yugoslavia, China, Cuba etc. remained bourgeois, i.e., that there was no qualitative difference between the state of Chiang Kai-shek and the state of Mao Zedong, between the state of Batista and the state of Fidel Castro. Again, a case of colour-blindness.

You don't need to love Mao Zedong or to transform him into a proponent of direct workers power or of socialist democracy, in order to grasp that genuine fundamental questions are involved here. Should revolutionists have been neutral in the civil war between Mihailović and the *Ustaše* on the one hand and Tito on the other hand? That would have been an openly counter-revolutionary position. Should the 'bourgeois' state of Mao Zedong be considered a 'lesser evil' compared to the bourgeois state of Chiang Kai-shek for political reasons? But Mao did not create any form of 'democratic' state. His state was a viciously dictatorial one. So whence the lesser evil?

Wouldn't critical support to the People's Liberation Army be justified precisely because we were confronted not with a political but with a social revolution, in which tens of millions of peasants (and quite a few workers too) fought against their class enemies, be it under a bureaucratic leadership? Wasn't the abolition of the comprador-landlord-imperialist rule a gigantic historical step forward for China? Or should one perhaps say that it was a 'side issue'?

The identification of genuine social revolutions with 'pure' leaderships, 'pure' ideologies and 'pure' forms, ends in the preposterously sectarian conclusion that no 'genuine' social revolution is possible without a conscious Marxist leadership, – thereby even denying the Paris Commune the nature of the dictatorship of the proletariat. Life has proven to be much more complex and much richer than the dogmatic schemas of such pedants.

The case of Cuba and Nicaragua is still clearer. By no stretch of imagination can one consider the Castro and Sandinista leaderships 'Stalinist' when they were conducting the civil war, with the enthusiastic support of the great majority of the toilers (including in Cuba an important urban proletariat which followed the call for a general strike by the Castro leadership).

In fact, they conducted their struggle against the strenuous and at times openly treacherous, counter-revolutionary opposition of the local Stalinists and the Kremlin. Would potential supporters of the 'state capitalist' dogma in Cuba and Nicaragua have fought on the side of the Fidelistas and the Sandinistas? Or should they have joined the Stalinist abstentionists, paraphrasing their argument that social revolutions were not on the agenda (with a different rationale: there is no genuine Marxist leadership)?

Or should they have striven as we advocated, to have the struggle for breaking the bourgeois army and the bourgeois state and suppressing at least large parts of private property? What was wrong with such an approach? Isn't that what actually did occur?[179]

Of course, we had to add to those demands that of the organization of a democratic workers state, based upon freely elected workers councils and multiparty democracy. But such a state did not exist anymore in Russia in 1922 either. Was Soviet Russia, therefore, a bourgeois state already in 1922?

The implications of these two different approaches in today's mass struggles in 'third world' countries are numerous. The defence of the specific immediate interests of the working class is a central element of our general strategy in 'third world' countries. But, after all, it was also a central piece of the Menshevik strategy in Russia too. That was not the main dividing line between Mensheviks and Bolshevism.

The main dividing line was the understanding, by the Bolsheviks, that the genuine and radical fight for the implementation of the national-democratic demands cannot be realised without a political break with the 'liberal' bourgeoisie and the fight for power.

The decisive addition to that position which is expressed in Trotsky's strategy of permanent revolution, and which has been thoroughly confirmed by nearly 80 years of historical experience (either positively, where it was applied, or negatively, where it was not), is that it is impossible to achieve the full realisation of the national-democratic tasks of emancipation (of the revolution) and a full break with the 'liberal' bourgeoisie, without pushing the emancipatory (revolutionary) process through to the point where you destroy the bourgeois army and the bourgeois state.

Whether you like it or not, that's what Tito, Mao, Castro and the Sandinistas did in practice, independently of their ideologies, initial intentions and later political developments. Anybody who wants to explain what really happened, and not stick to 'theories' completely unable to interpret reality, will have a hard time denying that obvious fact. This is even more true for the formula that these leaderships led these revolutions to victory 'under the pressure of the masses.' While that pressure was undeniable, it is not sufficient to explain what happened. It underestimates the key-role of the subjective factor and the undeniable merits of initiative and orientation of said bureaucratic leaderships.

Was there less pressure of the masses in Greece than in Yugoslavia? Yet in Greece the Stalinists saved the bourgeois state and gave up their weapons. In Yugoslavia, the CP led a popular revolution to the destruction of the bourgeois state and the bourgeois army. Again: was there less mass pressure in Indonesia than in Vietnam and in China in 1945-1949? Yet in Indonesia, the CP allowed the bourgeois army and the bourgeois state to retain power, which led to one million people killed by the counter-revolution. In China and Vietnam, the CP overthrew the bourgeois state through defeating the bourgeois army. Is that only a 'minor' difference?

Lack of genuine proletarian-democratic programme and

principle has disastrous results, sooner or later. But in order to build strong efficient genuinely proletarian-democratic revolutionary organizations in a revolutionary situation, you have to know in what camp you stand, with what arguments you operate and what is the hierarchy of your tasks.

Building the Fourth International or retreating into 'national communism'

Harman tries to justify the constitution of little groups in several countries, cloned on the British SWP, by referring to the need of having theory serve as a guide to action: without a correct theory, no correct action. So far, so good. He even points out to some good interventions which the followers of the SWP are supposed to have made in the general strikes in Greece and in the anti-fascist struggle in France.[180]

But the argument boomerangs: how can one seriously argue that you need the theory of state capitalism in order to understand the tasks with which revolutionary socialists are confronted in a general strike in Greece or in the anti-fascist struggle in France? Weren't these tasks also fulfilled by comrades who have different positions on the social nature of the USSR? Does not the same conclusion apply to Great Britain too?

What is the relevance of the theory of state capitalism existing in Russia to the anti-poll-tax struggle, to the struggle against Bush's and Major's Gulf War, to a correct assessment of what a Kinnock government would do to the working class, of what the attitude of British workers should be towards capitalist Europe, and to practically all problems of the immediate and future class struggle in Britain?

Harman accuses us of preferring to 'fudge' the question of the nature of Stalinism rather than precising it. We don't fudge that question. We make a more general point. We say that the programmatic questions on which advanced workers have to organize – and on which you have to build separate organizations – are the central problems of our epoch, the problems relating to world revolution, of overthrowing capitalism. On these questions you have to build separate organizations, lest the working class suffers terrible defeats nay lest humankind become annihilated. These questions turn around the key issue of how to prepare and organize the workers to take and exercise power in the economy and the state. Only inasmuch as the question of the nature of the USSR and of Stalinism is relevant to that central problem is it of vital importance.

So, it is Harman who is really fudging the issue. Is it justified, is it responsible to use the issue of state capitalism for the purpose of splitting revolutionary organizations intervening in current struggles, supporting and developing struggles for immediate and transitional demands, with the conscious purpose of preparing the ground for workers power? Is it responsible to subordinate the general movement towards the overthrow of capitalism to the special fight, to the state capitalist dogma? Isn't that exactly what Marx meant when he defined a sect as people addicted to their special *point d'honneur* instead of putting the general interests of the class first?

Precisely because of the predominant trend towards internationalization of capital and towards 'globalisation' of the key life-and-death questions, which confront humankind, the struggle for world revolution, for a Socialist World Federation, is the central issue for our epoch. Whatever the ups and downs of the class struggle, in the long run it too will become more and more international. It is totally utopian to believe the European working class, including the British working class, could meet the challenge of the EEC by retreating into self-defence measures on a national scale, in whatever form. Only the growing unity of action with the workers of the other European countries, with the workers of the rest of the world, can enable them to efficiently oppose the actions of the multinational corporations, inside Europe and outside Europe.

But in order to operate efficiently on an international scale, you need an international organization. We are no fetishists of the Fourth International as it is today. We know quite well that it is much too weak. We are in favour of a revolutionary mass International, composed of revolutionary mass parties in the key countries of the world. Of that future mass international, the present Fourth International will probably be only one of several components.

But that revolutionary mass international unfortunately does not yet exist. No important organization anywhere in the world, literally not a single one, is ready to put its creation immediately on the agenda. Under these circumstances no useful purpose can be served by giving up building the Fourth International. We shall continue to build it while at the same time facilitating all moves towards national and international regroupments of revolutionaries on a principled basis. As experience has shown building the Fourth International favours such regroupments, far from representing an obstacle to them.

You will not increase the consciousness of the need to proletarian internationalism basing itself upon an international organization, without showing in practice how such an organization can operate, should operate, and can develop. This is not in the first place an organizational question. It is certainly not a question of tactical choice. It is at the very heart of the Marxist programme and of the Marxist tradition.

It is sufficient to recall what Marx, Engels, Lenin, Rosa Luxemburg, Trotsky, Gramsci, Bukharin, and innumerable others wrote on that issue: 'The International is our real fatherland.'

You cannot be an advocate of international socialism and of world revolution and simultaneously put the building of the International off into the distant future as a secondary or even irrelevant question today. You cannot be an advocate of the strategy of permanent revolution and simultaneously relegate the building of the International to 'better times.' And you can especially not centre the building of an international organization on the issue of 'state capitalism', forgetting that such an International can only be built on the relevant class struggle problems of every country or at least most of the countries of the world.

Karl Marx historically summarized the reasons why you have to build simultaneously national parties and an International 120 years ago, in his Amsterdam speech of 1872:

Let us think of the basic principle of International Solidarity. Only when we have established this life-giving principle on a sound basis among the numerous workers of all countries will we attain the great final goal which we have set ourselves. The revolution must be carried out with great solidarity, this is the great lesson of the French Commune, which fell because none of the other centres – Berlin, Madrid etc – developed great revolutionary movements comparable to the mighty uprising of the Paris proletariat.

So far as I am concerned, I will continue my work and constantly strive to strengthen among all workers the solidarity that is so fruitful for the future. No, I do not withdraw from the International and all the rest of my life will be, as have been all my efforts of the past, dedicated to the triumph of the social ideas which – you be assured – will lead to the world domination of the proletariat.[181]

The great merit of the Fourth International as it exists, in spite of its weakness, is precisely that it does just that. It is the only existing organization which expresses the common and particular interests of the toilers in all countries – as we say in our jargon, 'in the three sectors of the world revolution', or of 'world reality' – and tries to unite them in practice.

There are a lot of people on the left in the West, the East and the South who enthusiastically support either the liberation struggles in the third world, or the mass struggles against the bureaucratic dictatorships in the East, or workers (and feminist and ecological) struggles in the West. But outside revolutionary Marxists, essentially the Fourth International, no political organization or current is ready to support all of them simultaneously, alike, without reservation, and without subordinating any of them to others. This is a very great source of strength. This creates a homogeneity in basic program and intervention much higher than anything the workers movement has known in the past.

The Fourth International hasn't been split in its basic attitude towards any war during the last three decades. Isn't that remarkable? Isn't that something new? Shouldn't that be recognized with genuine pride?

When we say that the Fourth International is still much too weak, we must add that it is quite stronger than what many people assume. Harman has got his membership figures wrong because he chalks up losses but forgets to add gains. The fact that the Fourth International is growing in a whole series of countries, on four continents – not in all countries, it is true – is quite significant in a world in which the left generally is in total disarray and steep decline. It proves that in our own modest and limited way, we already fill a need. Militants and organizations in various countries join us on the basis of their own class struggle experience, and the political and programmatic conclusions they draw therefrom. That is quite relevant to our debate, comrade Harman.

What the SWP is doing by refusing to join in that common effort is really retreating into 'national communism.' It has developed into a serious and relevant organization in Britain, but in Britain only. It is now saying in practice, never mind the verbal cover-up: our main purpose is to consolidate and expand the SWP erected upon the basis of the theory of state capitalism. To that purpose, we subordinate any effort of building the International. That is why we limit ourselves to cloning in some countries our own organization, refusing to link up with thousands of revolutionary socialists who have come to common programmatic and practical conclusions on the basis of their experience with the problems of class struggle with which they are confronted in their respective countries and internationally.

During the last months, the objective dialectic of 'national communism' has started to reveal itself dramatically in the case of two of the largest organizations claiming to be Trotskyist outside the Fourth International: the British 'Militant' group and the Argentine MAS (followers of Moreno).

In both of these organizations, sectors of its leadership suggested gravely erroneous national tactics as a result of a wrong assessment of the world situation and its impact on a national scale. They thought there was a rise of political mass radicalization of the working class on a national scale, whereas in reality there is a predominantly rightward political evolution of the class, under the impact of the worldwide capitalist offensive and the worldwide crisis of credibility of socialism, strong defensive mass struggles notwithstanding.

These wrong tactics brought parts of the 'Militant' and MAS leadership in head on collision with parts of the working class and of their own organizations' workers' basis.[182]

Any national grouping not sufficiently implanted in the international working class through membership and mass movements in an international organization really functioning as such, is condemned to make similar mistakes sooner or later. For it is condemned to elaborate analyses of world developments from behind office desks, by reading newspapers and books, without having these analyses checked and rechecked by political and organizational practice.

If you stick to your retreat into 'national communism' this will sooner or later lead to disaster in Britain too, comrades of the SWP. You cannot reach an adequate level of internationalist consciousness among your membership without an adequate level of international practice, which presupposes an adequate level of international organization.[183]

Let us illustrate our thesis by an 'extreme' example. Imagine a situation in which the workers of any country – yes, why not, including the Soviet Union – are unfolding mass struggles of such a scope that workers and popular councils are arising and that the question of their centralization is immediately on the agenda. Admittedly, this is not likely to happen in the immediate future. But the comrades of the SWP firmly believe, as we do, as all revolutionary Marxists do, that it will happen sooner or later, never mind the timescale.

Now add to that first hypothesis a second one: imagine that the great majority of the revolutionary socialists in that given country, actively struggling for that centralization of workers councils and preparing the working class for power, are opposed to the theory of state capitalism? Wouldn't it be irresponsible to the extreme, nay criminal, to split their forces on the issue of state capitalism and to weaken them in relation to all the opponents of workers power even at the eve of the struggle for power? Or would you seriously argue that it is impossible for the workers of that given country to take power without having first accepted the dogma of state capitalism?

One could answer: this is after all a moot question, for the direct struggle for workers power isn't on the agenda in any country just now (perhaps with a couple of exceptions). But this does not weaken our case. The struggle for workers power does not suddenly fall from the sky. It can only be the final link of a whole chain of intermediate links, experience and conclusions drawn by advanced workers first, broader masses later, from their current struggles, growing self-assurance and class consciousness assisted by adequate socialist propaganda and education.

In all these fields, the revolutionary organization's activity plays an important role. It is most probable that we shall not see workers councils emerge without previous experiences of elected strike committees and of their tendential centralization, that we shall not see revolutionary mass parties emerge without the revolutionary socialists increasing implantation and authority gained inside these initial forms of self-organization of the class as such.

Today's propaganda and incipient implementation of the central idea that socialism in the final analysis is self-activity and self-organization of the working class, is the struggle for democratically, i.e., pluralistically elected workers councils, is the struggle for democratically articulated self-management and planning in the economy, represents the only way to overcome the terrible crisis of credibility of socialism which all of us are confronted with worldwide. Do we stand in the same camp on that vital issue? If so, what is the purpose of not building together one International based upon it?

Trotsky's economic ideas and the Soviet Union today

Ernest Mandel

As the bureaucratic USSR sinks into chaos, the economic platform of Trotsky and the Left Opposition emerges as an indispensable guide to the relaunching of a socialist project. This explains why for the liberals the 'neo-Bolsheviks' are today the main enemy.

The disgraceful slanders hurled by Stalin and the neo-Stalinists against Leon Trotsky are today unanimously rejected in the USSR. On the eve of the fiftieth anniversary of his assassination the government daily *Izvestia* solemnly recognized that Lev Davidovich was a great and honest revolutionary, one of the principal founders and leaders of the Soviet state. Other newspapers have revealed that at two points during 1922 Lenin had proposed that Trotsky be vice president of the Council of People's Commissars and his designated successor in case of sickness or death.

But this is not to say that this rehabilitation of the founder of our movement signals an approval of his political platform which was opposed to that of Stalin. On the contrary. The media and social science circles in the USSR are dominated today by neo-social democratic and neo-liberal tendencies hostile to Leninism, to Marxism, and to the October revolution. For these currents, Trotsky remains an ideological adversary, Trotskyism a political enemy.

What is at stake, however, is an undeniable historical figure and tradition in the Soviet Union. It is difficult to deny that Stalin considered them as his number one enemy. As Stalin is hated by the immense majority of the Soviet people, it is necessary that the current ideologues work to prevent this hatred from translating automatically into a certain sympathy concerning Trotsky. The solution which they have generally opted for is that of raising a new set of slanders, less inflammatory than those of the Stalinists and neo-Stalinists, but founded just as much on open historical falsifications.

It is an historical irony that Trotsky is reproached today not for having been a counterrevolutionary but for having been an ultraleft 'revolutionary fanatic.' He is not reproached for having been an adversary of Lenin, but for having been, in 1917 and later, the damned soul and 'inspirer' of Lenin. Trotsky, the 'bloody' incarnation of the October revolution (a Jew and a 'cosmopolitan' imbued with 'European culture' to boot), is the prime target of the neo-fascists and the neo-Black Hundreds who are sometimes openly allied with the neo-Stalinists. According to all the 'democratic' opponents of the October revolution, Trotsky, the 'dogmatic utopian' of 'the historical mission of the working class,' was the greatest leader of the 'deviation' of Russian history from 1918 on.

An opponent of the NEP?

Within this cacophony the debate around economic alternatives occupies a key place. Trotsky is said to have been an opponent of the NEP [New Economic Policy], the partisan of 'super industrialization,' a fierce enemy of the private peasant, and the father of the 'command economy.' Stalin only applied Trotsky's economic program. The anti-Trotskyists in the USSR today say that the struggle between Stalin and Trotsky was simply a struggle for power between two despots.

This interpretation of the debate which swept the USSR from 1923 through 1928 all the way to 1934 involves a confusion between two distinct points of departure by Trotsky and the Left Opposition (not counting the capitulationists after 1929): The long-term analytical approach on the one hand, and the political approach operating on the immediate and medium term on the other. This confusion is the fruit of a deliberate lie, of ignorance, or of a lack of understanding about these questions.

In opposing the Stalinist theory that socialism could be achieved in one country, Trotsky affirmed his belief that, considering the nature of imperialism, whether socialism or capitalism would end up victorious in the Soviet Union could only be approached on an international scale. It was impossible to establish a true classless society of the 'freely associated producers' in Russia because this required a median level of labour productivity superior to that of the most advanced capitalist countries, but also in permanent conflict with the world capitalist market. The weight of this antagonism would end up by crushing the chances for socialism in the USSR by military or economic pressure if the revolution did not spread to the 'advanced capitalist nations.' This analysis of long-term trends certainly also had short-term implications. It underscored the dangers of a lagging development of industry which risked promoting an alliance between private Russian agriculture and the world capitalist market, a rupture of the worker-peasant alliance. To fight the dangers of capitalist restoration, it stressed the necessity of limiting the private accumulation of capital and of raising the productivity of state industry which would permit the sale of products at a lower price. This necessitated a more rapid development of industry.

Therefore, contrary to the legend of Stalinist-Bukharinist origin, developed in the 1960s by Georg Lukacs, Trotsky did not draw adventurist-defeatist conclusions from this analysis, which history has now confirmed in a striking way precisely on the economic plane. It in no way reduced the middle-term destiny of the Soviet Union to the dilemma of either a revolutionary war and territorial expansion or an inevitable retreat towards capitalism. On the contrary, he advanced the idea of a steady consolidation of the gains of the socialist revolution while waiting for the ripening of the objective and subjective conditions for revolutionary victories in the advanced countries. In other words, he proposed that the USSR enter the road of beginning to build socialism in a realistic and prudent manner without fanfare or illusions.

This 'Trotskyist' alternative was based on the dialectic of economic logic and on the dynamic of social forces. Trotsky's analysis remains unmatched among twentieth century Marxists. The acceleration of the rhythm of industrialization must proceed through the steady transfer of the social surplus towards the productive socialized sector of the economy, that is to say, essentially at the expense of the middle bourgeoisie (*kulaks* and *nepmen*) and at the expense of the bureaucracy, by a radical reduction of unproductive expenditures.

A reinforcement of the social weight of the proletariat and the poor peasantry in society (as well as a fraction of the middle peasantry ready to participate) had to be realized through the raising of their standard of living and an improvement of their working conditions: the elimination of unemployment; the leading role of workers in factory management; the recruitment of the working peasantry to production cooperatives founded from the start on mechanized labour in order to guarantee to its members returns higher than they had known as individual producers.

These proposals were marked by an internal coherence that is still impressive today. The building of the first large tractor factory in 1923 would have assured the 'voluntary participation of the poor peasants in the state farms.' It would have freed the towns from the danger of being of being blackmailed by reductions in deliveries from the rich peasants by preventing the concentration of the agricultural surplus in their hands. It would have allowed the continued raising of real wages that had proceeded until 1926-27. It would have provided the USSR with a powerful arms industry in order to defend itself from an eventual military attack over a ten-year rather than a five-year period.

At the same time this road of economic policy proposed to the Comintern and to the Communist parties would permit them to take full advantage of revolutionary situations like those which occurred between 1923-1937 in Germany, Great Britain, Spain, and France.

Far from being 'Trotskyism without Trotsky,' Stalinist economic policy from 1928 on was the antithesis of that advanced by the Opposition. Full-scale industrialization was accompanied by a lowering, not a raising of real wages, by a catastrophic deterioration, not an improvement of labour conditions. Administrative expenses were not reduced but colossally increased, absorbing the major part of what had been taken from worker consumption. This was the monstrous deadweight of the bureaucracy and its absolute power over society. If the rise in production could not be supported by the interests and consciousness of the producers, it must be realized by force and general control. In place of 'soviets everywhere' the reality was police control and red tape everywhere.

The forced collectivization of agriculture was the antithesis of the voluntary participation advocated by the Opposition, consistent with Lenin's 'cooperative plan.' It led to desperate resistance by the peasants, notably the massive slaughter of livestock. It was accompanied by a systematic underdevelopment of investments, in agriculture as much as in the service sector (stockpiling, transportation, distribution), and a fluctuating price policy. It was thus the source of misery in the countryside and poverty in the towns for decades.

Against the command economy

As soon as Stalin's policies became clear, Trotsky, Rakovsky, and the Left Opposition denounced the forced collectivization of agriculture, the total suppression of the NEP, 'super industrialization,' the attacks against real wages and peasant incomes, and the deepening of social inequality. To identify the Opposition with these policies, to hold that they inspired them, amounts therefore to a pure and simple lie. To identify the thesis of Preobrazhensky-Trotsky, according to which in the long term an extension of private appropriation of the social surplus and market mechanisms would make capitalist restoration inevitable, with the short – and medium-term elimination of these mechanisms is a falsification of the economic orientation of Trotsky and the Left Opposition. Several quotations will suffice to demonstrate this.

The opposition speaks
Christian Rakovsky, V. Kossior, N. Muralov, and V. Kasparova wrote in the declaration of 1930:

> *The decree that abolished the NEP and the kulaks as a class is ... an economic absurdity ... No charter, no decree can abolish the contradictions that still operate in the economy and in everyday life ... Attempts to ignore this economic truth... have led to the use of violence, breaking with the party's program, with the fundamental principles of Marxism and contempt for Lenin's most basic warnings concerning collectivization, the middle peasantry, and the NEP.*

On October 22, 1932, Trotsky continued in his article *The Soviet Economy in Danger*:

> *If a universal mind existed, of the kind that projected itself into the scientific fancy of Laplace – a mind that could register simultaneously all the processes of nature and society, that could measure the dynamics of their motion, that could forecast the results of their interactions – such a mind, of course, could a priori draw up a faultless and exhaustive economic plan, beginning with the number of acres of wheat down to the last button for a vest. The bureaucracy often imagines that just such a mind is at its disposal; that is why it so easily frees itself from the control of the market and of Soviet democracy. But, in reality, the bureaucracy errs frightfully in its estimate of its spiritual resources ... The innumerable living participants in the economy, state and private, collective and individual,*

must serve notice of their needs and of their relative strength not only through the statistical determinations of plan commissions but by the direct pressure of supply and demand. The plan is checked and, to a considerable degree, realized through the market. The regulation of the market itself must depend upon the tendencies that are brought out through its mechanism. The blueprints produced by the departments must demonstrate their economic efficiency through commercial calculation. The system of the transitional economy is unthinkable without the control of the rouble. This presupposes, in its turn, that the rouble is at par. Without a firm monetary unit, commercial accounting can only increase the chaos.[184]

He followed up on this in *The Revolution Betrayed*:

While the growth of industry and the bringing of agriculture into the sphere of state planning vastly complicates the tasks of leadership, bringing to the front the problem of quality, bureaucratism destroys the creative initiative and the feeling of responsibility without which there is not, and cannot be, qualitative progress. The ulcers of bureaucratism are perhaps not so obvious in the big industries, but they are devouring, together with the cooperatives, the light – and food-producing industries, the collective farms, the small local industries – that is, all those branches of economy which stand nearest to the people ...

It is possible to build gigantic factories according to a ready-made Western pattern by bureaucratic command – although, to be sure, at triple the normal cost. But the farther you go, the more the economy runs into the problem of quality, which slips out of the hands of a bureaucracy like a shadow. The Soviet products are as though branded with the grey label of indifference. Under a nationalized economy, quality demands a democracy of producers and consumers, freedom of criticism and initiative – conditions incompatible with a totalitarian regime of fear, lies, and flattery.[185]

Three orientations

There were three distinct currents of economic policy in the CPSU between 1928 and 1934, assuming the supporters of Bukharin remained so after 1933, which is not at all certain.

- Stalin's line was founded on the forced collectivization of agriculture and super industrialization at the expense of the workers and peasants, and ultra-centralized and ultra-disproportionate planning (or rather semi-planning).

- Bukharin's line was based on the 'peaceful coexistence' of the private and socialized economy, the former being charged with providing for the latter whose expansion would remain sharply limited.

- The Opposition's line foresaw a more rapid expansion of the socialized sector than Bukharin's plan, but much less rapid and certainly more balanced than Stalin's. It called for the reduction of unproductive expenses like those appropriated by the bureaucracy as well as the improvement of the lives of workers and working peasants.

These three currents clearly reflected the pressure of different social forces. But it must be remembered that, at least during the period from 1930-33, the differences between the concrete proposals of the Opposition and those of the Bukharinists were much less clear than with those of Stalin.

What characterized the economic program of the Opposition more than anything else was the unity and clarity of its economic positions on the one hand and its political and social positions on the other: soviet democracy, satisfaction of the material demands of the producers, the struggle against inequality and bureaucratic privileges.

In 1932, also in *The Soviet Economy in Danger*, Trotsky declared that:

The struggle between living interests, as the fundamental factor of planning, leads us into the domain of politics, which is concentrated economics. The instruments of the social groups of Soviet society are – should be: the Soviets, the trade unions, the cooperatives, and in first place the ruling party. Only through the interaction of these three elements, state planning, the market, and Soviet democracy, can the correct direction of the economy of the transitional epoch be attained.[186]

This last sentence deserves to be underlined. And in *The Revolution Betrayed*, Trotsky held that:

A restoration of the right of criticism and a genuine freedom of elections are necessary conditions for the further development of the country. This assumes a revival of freedom of Soviet parties, beginning with the party of Bolsheviks, and a resurrection of the trade unions. The bringing of the democracy into industry means a radical revision of plans in the interests of the toilers. Free discussion of economic problems will decrease the overhead expense of bureaucratic mistakes and zigzags. Expensive playthings – palaces of the Soviets, new theatres, show-off subways – will be crowded out in favour of workers' dwellings. 'Bourgeois norms of distribution' will be confined within the limits of strict necessity, and in step with the growth of social wealth, will give way to socialist equality.[187]

These lines written fifty-five years ago retain a burning relevance in today's USSR. Once again, we find three fundamentally different currents of economic policy:

- The first is to maintain the bureaucratic control over the economy at the price of important economic reforms.

- The second aims at developing important private sector with encouragement given to the primitive accumulation of capital.

- The third is a neo-socialist defence of the immediate interests of the workers (full employment, increased buying power, social services) and the reduction of social injustices and inequalities.

The second tendency, in contradiction to that of Bukharin and his comrades who were honest communists, is essentially anti-communist and anti-socialist. The third is not Trotskyist. But it must increasingly borrow from the ideas of revolutionary Marxism, regardless of the vocabulary it chooses, in order for it to join hands with the real independent workers' movement currently reviving in the USSR.

New slanders

It is noteworthy that a pro-capitalist and liberal opponent of Bolshevism, Leonid Radzikhovski, writing in the September 9 issue of the *Moscow News*, accuses both neo-Stalinists like Nina Andreyevna and comrade Buzgalin, spokesman of the 'Marxist Platform' in the CPSU, of being inspired by Trotsky's ideas – putting them in the same bag in the best Stalinist tradition. 'Neo-Bolsheviks' are thus all 'neo-Trotskyists.' However, the same Radzikhovski had to recognize that:

> *Thanks to his Marxist analysis, Trotsky discovered the principal evil in Soviet society: The struggle of a new aristocracy, of the bureaucracy against the popular masses who brought it to power ... Trotsky also developed in the 1930s a program for reorganizing the Soviet Union that involved democratization, self-management, openness, and even the market.*

Exactly. But to accuse the new Soviet socialist left of wanting to 'defend the bureaucratic system against capitalism' is a gross slander. Like Trotsky, the true 'neo-Bolsheviks' fight on two fronts: Against the bureaucracy and against the rising middle bourgeoisie. That is consistent with the workers' material interests.

The supreme contradiction that the neo-liberals face is the following: How can the majority of citizens be prevented from defending their own interests while the sacred right of every individual is proclaimed? In the name of what principle? Could it be, in the best Stalinist tradition, that the people must be made to be happy in spite of and against itself by the use of force?

The laws of motion of the Soviet economy

Ernest Mandel

To the extent that one can discover general laws for the existing societies in transition between capitalism and socialism, which are characterized by extreme bureaucratic deformation or degeneration, they would have to be characterized as follows:

1. State ownership of all important industrial, transportation and financial enterprises (i.e., of the means of production and circulation), combined with legal (constitutional) suppression of the right to their private appropriation, centralized economic planning and state monopoly of foreign trade, imply the absence of generalized commodity production and the *rule* of the law of value in the USSR. This means that the economy is no longer capitalist. There is neither a market for large means of production nor for manpower, and labour-power has ceased to be a commodity.

   On the other hand, the pressure of the world market, the insufficient level of development of the productive forces, the conflict of interest between social classes (workers, peasants) and social layers (the bureaucracy), the enormous structural differences between industry and agriculture, town and countryside, manual and intellectual labour[188] lead to an inevitable survival of commodity production – essentially of means of consumption[189]– and to the impossibility of freeing the economy completely of value. The survival of a partial commodity production implies that the economy is not yet a socialist one. The unfolding conflict between the logic of the plan and the influence of the law of value is therefore the main contradiction and the main law of motion of the Soviet economy, as of all economies in the phase of transition between capitalism and socialism.

2. The absence of the *rule* of the law of value implies, among other things, that the Soviet economy has been able to develop independently from the profit-derived sector priorities and distortions imposed by international capitalism on all less developed economies in the epoch of imperialism. It also implies that it has been able to avoid the business cycle, periodic crises of overproduction, and conjunctural large-scale unemployment. It has been characterized by long-term average rates of growth superior to those of industrialized capitalist countries, even after achieving its basic industrialization. But the survival of partial commodity production, the pressure of the world market and all the other constraints mentioned above, objectively restrict the efficiency and scope of global economic planning. They imply periodic fluctuations in the rate of economic growth and a series of tensions and crises specific to a society in transition between capitalism and socialism, qualitatively different from both the capitalist and socialist economy. They also imply the possibility of partial overproduction of all those goods which remain commodities.

3. Survival of commodity production in Department II – and its correlative, the money or wage-form of redistribution of labour-power (the workers' access to consumer goods mainly through exchange against money) – implies for every society in transition between capitalism and socialism

a contradiction between non-capitalist relations of production and bourgeois forms of distribution.[190] This conflict is not restricted to the sphere of distribution only. It has repercussions in the sphere of production, in the organization of work and production relations at a plant level, and in the techniques of planning. One of these repercussions is a bias towards independent book-keeping at enterprise level and, as a result of the generalized use of money for national book-keeping, a bias towards financial autonomy of enterprises. So long as only partial commodity production survives, money does not and cannot have the same functions as under capitalism or even under petty commodity production; it cannot become large-scale capital, and only in marginal cases ('black market production') does it become a means of direct exploitation of labour-power. But though never an instrument for really appropriating large means of production, it *can* become a means of *partial* private appropriation of the social surplus product (interest, rent) and it *does* unleash a spontaneous tendency to primitive private capital accumulation, up to a certain ceiling. It remains especially a key vehicle for the consolidation and transmission of social inequality (inheritance). This is another key contradiction and law of motion of the Soviet economy.

4. These basic contradictions, characteristic for *all* social formations in transition between capitalism and socialism, are greatly aggravated in the USSR by the political counter-revolution (Thermidor) which triumphed in the Twenties, and which led to a monopoly of power (administration) in all spheres of social life by a materially privileged social layer, the bureaucracy. In the same way as the law of value reigns in its most normal, least impeded way under competitive capitalism, socially planned investment and distribution of the main economic resources function in a normal and unimpeded way only under the control and management of the economy by the associated producers themselves. Management of productive units and of all basic economic processes by a privileged bureaucracy necessarily introduces

enormous distortions and waste in the planning process, which combine with those distortions arising from the survival of partial commodity production, the pressure of the world market, etc., and strengthen them constantly. These distortions account for many of the specific crises which the Soviet economy has witnessed during the past half-century. This is another basic law of motion of the Soviet economy.

5. The mass of the producers have an evident *dual* interest in optimizing the planned use of economic resources: their interest in minimizing their (mechanical, non-creative) labour inputs, and their interest in minimizing their consumer satisfaction.[191] Any waste of economic resources violates one or both of these interests. There is no empirical evidence or theoretical 'proof' that under real democratic workers' management, a centrally planned collectivized economy would not allow a more efficient combination of economic resources than that achieved through competition and attempts at profit maximization under capitalism.

But in the absence of democratic control over planning, production and distribution by the associated producers themselves, the only way in which a centrally planned collectivized economy can be run is by a (contradictory) combination of the drive for material self-interest by the 'managerial' layer of the bureaucracy, and of political control by the state apparatus (the party apparatus having long since been absorbed by the state apparatus). Experience has confirmed what Marxist theory could predict: such a combination *must* keep the development of Soviet economy constantly *below* its optimum rate of growth, and *must* periodically produce explosive disproportions between different branches of the national economy. This is again a basic law of motion of the Soviet economy.

6. The material privileges of the bureaucracy are essentially restricted to the spheres of consumption. (We leave aside 'immaterial privileges,' 'social prestige,' the 'thirst for power' not expressed in material advantages, which are irrelevant to economic analysis.) Given the specific nature

of the Soviet economy, these privileges take two forms: higher money incomes (including those illegally acquired through bribes, corruption, theft, 'grey' and 'black' market operations, etc.), and non-monetary advantages linked to given hierarchical levels inside the bureaucracy (access to special shops, to state-owned cars, apartments, dachas, etc.). Both forms lead to a qualitatively higher access to consumer goods (of higher quality) than that of the average worker (not to speak of the average peasant). But they do not lead to private ownership of the means of production, nor to the accumulation of huge private money fortunes.

This introduces an additional, and explosive, contradiction into the functioning of the Soviet economy. While the material self-interest of the bureaucracy is the main instrument for the realization of the plan (the main mechanism through which economic growth is socially mediated, given the bureaucracy's monopoly of administration of the economy), there is no economic mechanism, not to speak of a spontaneously or automatically functioning one, through which the fulfilment of that self-interest can dovetail with the optimization of economic growth – at least not from the moment a certain threshold of industrialization has been passed. (Incidentally, this is one of the main theoretical proofs that the bureaucracy is not the new ruling class).[192]

All the main economic reforms of the Soviet economy since the Second Five-Year Plan – from the *khozraschyot* principle introduced under Stalin, to Khrushchev's *sovnarkhozy*, Lieberman's proposed 'restoration of the profit indicator of overall economic performance,' – and Kosygin's system of 'combined indicators' – are unsuccessful attempts to overcome that contradiction which fuels another basic law of motion of the Soviet economy. They *must* remain unsuccessful, because by its very nature as a *material* privileged layer in consumption, the bureaucracy *cannot* overcome its tendency to subordinate overall social priorities to *private* sectoral advantages (calculated by and gained for the management of each separate factory, trust, locality, region, branch, nationality, etc.). Only democratically associated producers receiving an *equalized 'social dividend'* from increased economic growth or increased productivity of labour, would be genuinely interested in global social optimization of the use of economic resources.

Any form of bureaucratic management will, therefore, always lead to a waste of such resources, e.g., hiding reserves, transmitting false information, excessive input requirements, outputs of low quality or unrelated to consumer needs, under-employment of productive capacity, theft of productive inputs for 'grey' or 'black market' operations, etc. Neither the systematic use of terror (as under Stalin) nor the partial restoration of market mechanisms can eliminate the source of that waste, which is the conflict between the material private self-interest of the managing bureaucracy and the needs of optimum use of economic resources made possible by the abolition of private ownership of the means of production and of the rule of the law of value, and demanded by the collective interests of the overwhelming majority of the producers. (It is obvious that each successive bureaucratic reform *can* achieve, and has achieved, *some* temporary, partial success in overcoming particularly heavy blocks to further economic growth.)

7. The tremendous cumulative growth of the Soviet economy over more than half a century, made possible by the overthrow of capitalism, has transformed that country from a relatively backward one into the second largest industrial power on earth, at least from the point of view of total absolute production figures. It has even permitted industrial productivity of labour to approach the levels of Italy and Britain, while agricultural productivity of labour remains dismally low. This economic growth has dramatically increased the social weight of the Soviet proletariat, its level of culture and technical skill. The objective possibilities of workers' management of the economy are today incomparably higher than they were in 1917, 1927 or 1937.

    However, none of this implies that the more the Soviet economy grows the easier and quicker becomes the overthrow of the bureaucracy's monopoly of power and management of the economy and society. The relative stability of its rule which has lasted much longer than most Marxist critics thought possible, can be explained by the fact that this overthrow can result only from conscious political action, i.e., a political revolution, which requires not only ripe objective conditions but also ripe subjective conditions. The relative unripeness of these latter is the key reason for the relative longevity of bureaucratic dictatorship.

8. On the one hand, one of the main results of the long period of dictatorship (especially under Stalin's reign of terror, but not only under these conditions) has been a process of progressive atomisation and de-politicization of the Soviet working class, which has put big subjective obstacles in the path of a political revolution. The way in which communism, Marxism, and socialism have become discredited in the eyes of the Soviet proletariat, as a result of their systematic prostitution as an apologetic state religion in the service of the bureaucracy, is typical of these new subjective obstacles. This is especially so in the absence of a victorious socialist revolution in the West or of a victorious political revolution in an Eastern European country, which could offer the Soviet workers a more attractive 'alternative model for the building of socialism' than the Stalinist one.

On the other hand, the very growth of the Soviet economy, in spite of all the waste caused by bureaucratic mismanagement, has created the basis for a slow but steady long-term improvement in the standard of living of the Soviet workers, which is now much higher than it was. The Soviet bureaucracy can therefore embark upon a course of 'reformist consumerism' as an alternative to political action inside the Soviet working class. While such a course provokes new tensions and contradictions, arising from unsatisfied rising expectations (for quality consumer goods, access to higher education, a better health service, freedom to travel abroad, etc.) it has, at least for a period, maintained depoliticization and atomization inside the working class and has hampered a rebirth of systematic mass action or mass organization (except, in part, among oppressed nationalities, and then for national goals only).

But the relative unripeness of the subjective preconditions for political revolution does not lead either to a smooth reproduction of bureaucratic rule or to automatic economic growth. It introduces another partially explosive contradiction into the Soviet economy. The more the growing objective weight of the Soviet proletariat collides with its continuous elimination from meaningful decision-taking processes in management and planning, the more a *generalized indifference towards the outcome of the productive process* permeates all levels of workers' activities, and this in turn becomes a major source of slow-down in economic growth (and a huge reserve source of additional growth in the event of a victorious political revolution).

9. For twenty years, the Soviet bureaucracy has confronted growing problems arising from the need to pass from extensive to intensive industrialization. This need results from the gradual exhaustion of the large-scale reserves in land, agricultural labour and raw materials which had been available for industrialization during the first decades after the initiation of the Five-Year Plans. All attempts to solve these problems till now have failed to achieve a qualitatively higher degree of efficiency in the use of economic resources, though some progress continues to be achieved. The two basic stumbling blocks which the Bonapartist leadership of the bureaucracy cannot overcome are the impossibility (already mentioned) of rationally tying the material self-interests of the bureaucracy to the optimization of economic growth, and the impossibility (already mentioned) of overcoming the relative indifference towards production of the direct producers. The first of these could be overcome only through re-establishing a permanent tie of material interests between the individual bureaucrats and given enterprises, i.e., re-introducing private property in the economic (and not necessarily at the same moment in the juridical) sense

of the term, i.e., through a restoration of capitalism. The second stumbling block could be overcome only through the conquest of generalized workers' control, workers' management, and workers' political power in the economy and society. The first of these radical changes would mean a victorious social counterrevolution, the second a victorious political antibureaucratic revolution.

10. Inside the bureaucracy, especially its 'managerial' wing, there is undoubtedly a tendency towards linking its drive for security of social status, income and privileges to *permanent* ties with a given enterprise or group of enterprises. This tendency reflects the general historical experience that without such ties (i.e., private property in the economic sense of the term), no permanent guarantee can be found for the security of material privileges and social status and their transmission to the next generations. This tendency dovetails with the objective trend of the dictatorship to try to find a unifying *rationale* between the material self-interests of the bureaucrats and the need to streamline the operation of the system. It likewise dovetails with the pressure of the world market, the trend towards private small-scale primitive capital accumulation, the operation of 'grey' and 'black market' sectors of production, etc. If successful, it would lead by degrees to a disappearance of central planning, a dismantling of the state monopoly of foreign trade and to a growing symbiosis of a certain number of Soviet enterprises – freed from the iron control of the plan – with their counterparts in imperialist countries.

But before such tendencies could lead to a restoration of capitalism, they would have to eliminate the resistance of the key sectors of the state apparatus which oppose that trend. This, incidentally, is the objective justification for the use of the scientific formula 'degenerated workers state' for the Soviet state, in spite of all its anti-working class measures and the total lack of direct class power or even political rights in the USSR. They would especially have to break the resistance of the working class itself which would stand to lose, as a result of such a process of capitalist restoration, the principal remaining conquest of the October revolution in its own eyes: a qualitatively higher degree of job security than under capitalism (the right to work).[193] Restoration of capitalism on the 'cold' or gradual road (as imagined through a 'palace revolution,' by the Maoists, Bettelheim and other theoreticians) is as impossible as the overthrow of capitalism in a gradual way. To believe otherwise is, to use an apt formula of Trotsky's, 'to unwind the reformist movie backwards.' Such a restoration could result only from new and disastrous defeats of the Soviet and international proletariat, after violent social and political confrontations. These are still before us, not behind us.

11. The overthrow of capitalism in a number of East European countries after World War II, as a result of military-bureaucratic interventions by the Soviet state, has created a Kremlin-controlled *glacis* at the Western frontier of the USSR over which the Soviet bureaucracy exercises a far-reaching control. But while that control was nearly unlimited during the first years after the upheaval and during the cold war period, it has gradually become more contradictory under the – sometimes combined, sometimes autonomous – operations of the three major factors: in each of those countries a ruling 'national' bureaucratic layer has emerged which has its own material interests to defend and which, while ultimately depending on the Soviet army to guarantee its rule, can up to a certain point haggle with the Kremlin over the degree of 'national autonomic economic development' and can put innumerable stumbling blocks in the road to greater integration inside COMECON. (The Rumanian bureaucracy is the prototype of such a 'national' bureaucracy.) Each of these countries (with the possible exception of Bulgaria) is much more dependent upon foreign trade with the capitalist countries, and is therefore much more vulnerable than the Soviet economy to the fluctuations of the international capitalist economy. This also has social and political

consequences inside those countries; especially in those where the degree of atomization and political passivity of the working class is much less than in the USSR. Indeed, in four of these countries (GDR 1953, Hungary and Poland 1956, Czechoslovakia 1968) we have already witnessed the beginning of huge mass movements centred around the working class and leading to the very threshold of political revolution.

Objective economic needs make unavoidable a gradual growing integration of the Soviet economy with those of the 'people's democracies.' But the Soviet bureaucracy cannot finalize such an integration beyond a given threshold, and each attempt unleashes further powerful contradictions, especially if it conflicts with the immediate interests of the masses: for in that case a higher level of working-class activity and consciousness in Eastern Europe is transferred (at least partially and temporarily) into the Soviet economy and society. This has become an additional and important law of motion of the Soviet economy.

12. The laws of motion of Soviet economy and society are inextricably linked to the class struggle on a world scale, i.e., to the outcome of the historical conflict between the world proletariat and the international capitalist class, i.e., to the fate of world revolution and of the international capitalist system. The victory of the October socialist revolution in a relatively backward country is in the last analysis understandable only against the background of the decline beginning of the world capitalist system in the imperialist epoch. Historically, it signifies the beginning of the process of world revolution.

The counter-revolutionary victory of Stalinism, the establishment of the bureaucratic dictatorship in the USSR. is ultimately the result of grave defeats of world revolution, of which the defeat of the Russian proletariat by the bureaucratic onslaught was an important part. But the survival of the USSR. as a non-capitalist economy and society (in spite of three powerful attempts at capitalist restoration by imperialism in 1918-1921, in 1941-1944 and in 1947-1951) is the result of the fact that the Stalinist counter-revolutionary victories were only partial, that the world proletariat was not completely defeated and reduced to passivity, that the historical crisis of the capitalist mode of production was itself too powerful an obstacle to be overcome, and that periodic new upsurges of world revolution occurred after the early forties.

In that sense, the future of the Soviet Union is yet undecided. Its fate depends upon the outcome of the struggle between antagonistic class forces on a world scale. Precisely because the Soviet economy is not a new mode of production, definitely crystallized and capable of autonomous self-reproduction, its inner laws of motion in and by themselves cannot decide its final form. New decisive defeats of the international proletariat will give a powerful impulse to a restoration of capitalism in the USSR. Any decisive victory of world revolution will give a powerful impulse to a victory of the politically antibureaucratic revolution in the Soviet Union, and will reopen the road to socialism which the bureaucratic dictatorship has blocked.

Sources

Revolutionary Marxism and late Soviet realities, Ernest Mandel's confrontation with state capitalist theory – Paul Le Blanc
Introduction written especially for this volume.

From Trotsky to state capitalism – Chris Harman
First published in *International Socialism*, no. 47, Summer 1990. Published in *Fallacies of state capitalism* (London: Socialist Outlook, November 1991). 'From Trotsky to state capitalism' was a review of Ernest Mandel: *Beyond Perestroika*, London: Verso, 1989. Transcribed by Christian Høgsbjerg. Marked up by Einde O'Callaghan for the *Marxists' Internet Archive*.

A theory which has not withstood the test of facts
– Ernest Mandel
First published in *International Socialism*, no. 49, Winter 1990. Published in *Fallacies of state capitalism* (London: Socialist Outlook, November 1991). 'A theory which has not withstood the test of facts', is a reply to 'From Trotsky to state capitalism' by Chris Harman. Translated by Gareth Jenkins. Copied from the blog *Chris Harman's Back Pages*. Marked up by Einde O'Callaghan for the *Marxists' Internet Archive*.

Criticism which does not withstand the test of logic. A reply to Ernest Mandel – Chris Harman
First published in *International Socialism*, no.49, Winter 1990. Published in *Fallacies of state capitalism* (London: Socialist Outlook, November 1991). The article is a reply to 'A theory which has not withstood the test of facts' by Ernest Mandel. Originally copied from the blog *Chris Harman's Back Pages* by Jørn Andersen for *Marxisme Online*. Copied with thanks from *Marxisme Online*. Marked up by Einde O'Callaghan for the *Marxists' Internet Archive*.

The impasse of schematic dogmatism – Ernest Mandel
First published in *Fallacies of state capitalism* (London:
Socialist Outlook, November 1991). An edited version was
published in *International Socialism* no.56, Autumn 1992.

**Trotsky's economic ideas and the Soviet Union today
– Ernest Mandel**
First published with the title 'L'alternative economique'
in a special issue of *Rouge*, the newspaper of the *Ligue
Communiste Revolutionnaire* (LCR), French section of the
Fourth International. It was published to commemorate the
fiftieth anniversary of the assassination of Leon Trotsky in
August 1990. It was published in English in the *Bulletin in
Defense of Marxism*, no. 84, April 1991. The translation from
the French is by Kay Mann. It was transcribed by Joe Auciello
and marked up by Einde O'Callaghan for the *Marxists Internet
Archive*. Downloaded with thanks from the *Ernest Mandel
Internet Archive*.

The Laws of Motion of the Soviet Economy – Ernest Mandel
First published in *The Review of Radical Political Economics*,
vol. 13, no.1, Spring 1981, pp. 35-39. It was transcribed by
Joe Auciello and marked up by Einde O'Callaghan for the
Marxists Internet Archive. Downloaded with thanks from
the *Ernest Mandel Internet Archive*.

Notes

1   *Marxist Economic Theory*, 2 vols. (New York: Monthly Review Press, 1968), *The Formation of the Economic Thought of Karl Marx* (New York: Monthly Review Press, 1971), *Late Capitalism* (London: Verso, 1975), *Long Waves of Capitalist Development* (London: Verso, 1995), *Trotsky, A Study in the Dynamic of His Thought* (London: New Left Books, 1979), *Trotsky as Alternative* (London: Verso, 1995). Mandel's life and ideas are discussed in Jan Willem Stutje, *Ernest Mandel, A Rebel's Dream Deferred* (London: Verso, 2009), and Gilbert Achcar, ed., *The Legacy of Ernest Mandel* (London: Verso, 1999). Additional information and writings are available in the Ernest Mandel Internet Archive: www.ernestmandel.org/en/index.html, and in the Marxist Internet Archive: https://www.marxists.org/archive/mandel/.

2   An informative collection of remembrances on Harman can be found in the journal *International Socialism* #125, Winter 2010, also available online: isj.org.uk/issue-125/. Writings and information can also be found through the Marxist Internet Archive: www.marxists.org/archive/harman/index.htm.

3   In a 1979 interview, Tony Cliff commented that his state-capitalist theory originated with the notion that 'if the emancipation of the working class is the act of the working class, then you cannot have a workers' state without the workers having power to dictate what happens in society,' as cited in Marcel van der Linden, *Western Marxism and the Soviet Union* (Haymarket Books, 2009), p. 119.

4   Ernest Mandel, *Beyond Perestroika: The Future of Gorbachev's USSR* (London: Verso, 1989); Ernest Mandel, *Money and Power, A Marxist Theory of Bureaucracy* (London: Verso, 1992).

5   See essays and materials in Paul Le Blanc, Ernest Mandel, David Mandel, Rosa Luxemburg and V.I. Lenin, *October 1917, Workers in Power* (London: Resistance Books/International Institute for Research and Education/Merlin Press, 2017). An intensive examination of complex and problematical developments is offered in Paul Le Blanc, *October Song: Bolshevik Triumph, Communist Tragedy 1917-1924* (Chicago: Haymarket Books, 2017). Surveys of the history can be found in Ronald Grigor Suny, *The Soviet Experiment: Russia, the USSR, and the Successor States* (New York: Oxford University Press, 1998) and Moshe Lewin, *The Soviet Century* (London: Verso, 2016).

6   The range of prominent thinkers and activists is indicated in Ernest Mandel, ed., *Fifty Years of World Revolution 1917-1967, An International Symposium* (New York: Merit Publishers, 1968).

A sympathetic overview of the Fourth International can be found in Pierre Frank, *The Fourth International: The Long March of the Trotskyists* (London: Ink Links, 1979), with much additional detail to be found in the massive and more critical Robert J. Alexander, *International Trotskyism 1929-1985: A Documentary Analysis of the Movement* (Durham, NC: Duke University Press, 1991). A rich first-hand account can be found in Livio Maitan, *Memoirs of a Critical Communist: Towards a History of the Fourth International* (London: Resistance Books/International Institute for Research and Education/Merlin Press, 2019).

7   On the birth and development of this current, see Tony Cliff et al, *The Origins of the International Socialists* (London: Pluto Press, 1971) and Ian Birchall's splendid biography *Tony Cliff, A Marxist for His Time* (London: Bookmarks, 2011), the key work being Tony Cliff, *State Capitalism in Russia* (London: Bookmarks, 1988). The Cliff group's 1950 characterization of the Fourth International terms it 'bankrupt politically, capitulating to Stalinism and Titoism, lacking any consistent policy toward reformism, showing all the signs of bureaucratic degeneration' (Birchall, p. 134).

8   Marcel van der Linden, *Western Marxism and the Soviet Union* (Chicago: Haymarket Books, 2009), pp. 302, 305, 313, 318. It should be noted that adherents of the 'bureaucratic-collectivist' current sharply divided between those like Max Shachtman who supported U.S. foreign policy and others like Hal Draper who rejected that path and remained equally critical of both sides in the Cold War. See Peter Drucker, *Max Shachtman and His Left, A Socialist's Odyssey through the 'American Century'* (Atlantic Highlands, NJ: Humanities Press, 1994), and Hal Draper, *Socialism from Below* (Chicago: Haymarket Books, 2019).

9   Van der Linden, pp. 49-63, 107-126, 160-161, 180-192, 258-280, 309; Erich Farl, 'The State Capitalist Genealogy,' *International*, vol. 2, no. 1, Spring 1973, pp. 18-23.

10   Thomas M. Twiss, *Trotsky and the Problem of Soviet Bureaucracy* (Chicago: Haymarket Books, 2015). Also see Kunal Chattopadhyay's massive study, *The Marxism of Leon Trotsky* (Kolkata: Progressive Publishers, 2006).

11   This section of my discussion draws from Paul Le Blanc, 'Trotsky and the Democratic Struggle in the USSR,' *Bulletin in Defense of Marxism*, December 1991, pp. 8-11.

12   Robert H. McNeal, 'Trotskyist Interpretations of Stalinism,' in Robert C. Tucker, ed., *Stalinism* (New York: W.W. Norton, 1977), pp. 31, 30.

13   Leon Trotsky, *The Revolution Betrayed, What is the Soviet Union and Where is It Going?* (Garden City, NY: Doubleday, Doran & Co., 1937), pp. 6, 8.

14   Ibid., pp. 53, 56.

15   Ibid., p. 96.

16   Ibid., p. 100.

17   Ibid., p. 112. (The translation is slightly modified here.)

18   Ibid., p. 255.

19   Ibid., pp. 277-278.

20   Ibid., pp. 278-279.

21   Ibid., p. 254.

22   Ibid., pp. 274, 275. For an overview of Soviet economic development, see Alec Nove, *An Economic History of the USSR: 1917-1991*, 3rd Edition (Penguin, 1993).

23   Trotsky, *The Revolution Betrayed*, pp. 275,276.

24   Catherine Samary, 'Mandel's Views on the Transition to Socialism,' in Achcar, p. 169.

25   On the short-lived liberalizing 'good years' and the horror that followed, see: Ronald Grigor Suny, *The Soviet Experiment: Russia, the USSR and the Successor States* (New York: Oxford University Press, 1998), pp. 247, 257-268; Robert C. Tucker, *Stalin in Power: The Revolution from Above, 1928-1941* (New York: W. W. Norton, 1990), pp. 238-254, 271-337, 366-478; Oleg V. Khlevniuk, *Stalin, New Biography of a Dictator* (New Haven: Yale University Press, 2015), pp. 122-141, 150-162.

26   Trotsky, *The Revolution Betrayed*, p. 287.

27   Ibid., pp. 250-251.

28   Ibid., pp. 285, 286.

29   My own summary description of the Soviet Left Opposition before and during its destruction can be found in Paul Le Blanc, *Leon Trotsky* (London: Reaktion Books, 2015), pp. 117-125. Eyewitness accounts are provided in: Maria Joffe, *One Long Night* (London: New Park Publications, 1978); Joseph Berger, *Shipwreck of a Generation* (London: Harvill Press, 1971), pp. 82-98; George Saunders [Shriver], ed., *Samizdat: Voices of the Soviet Opposition* (New York: Monad Press/Pathfinder Press 1974), pp. 61-181, 206-216; and Victor Serge, *Russia Twenty Years After* New Edition (Atlantic Highlands, NJ: Humanities Press, 1996), pp. 94-123. Richly informative accounts can also be found in Pierre Broué, 'The Bolshevik-Leninist Faction,' *Revolutionary History*, vol. 9, no. 4, 2007, and information-packed volumes by Vadim Z. Rogovin, *Bolsheviks Against Stalinism 1928-1933: Trotsky and the Left Opposition* (Oak Park, MI: Mehring Books, 2019) and *1937: Stalin's Year of Terror* (Oak Park, MI: Mehring Books, 1998).

30   Trotsky, *The Revolution Betrayed*, pp. 282, 283.

31   Ibid., p. 284.

32   Trotsky, *The Revolution Betrayed*, pp. 252, 289, 290.

33   Ibid., p. 252.

34   Ibid., p. 289.

35   Ibid., pp. 253, 252, 289.

36   Ibid., pp. 290, 300- 301, 291.

37   'The Death Agony of Capitalism and the Tasks of the Fourth International,' in Will Reisner, ed., *Documents of the Fourth International, The Formative Years 1933-40* (New York: Pathfinder Press, 1973), pp. 219-220.

38   Jürgen Kocka, *Capitalism, A Short History* (Princeton, NJ: Princeton University Press, 2016), pp. 25, 53, 54, 95-159.

39   Ibid., p. viii. Such conceptualizations seem similar to analyses in Jairus Banaji, *Theory as History: Essays on Modes of Production and Exploitation* (Chicago: Haymarket Books, 2011).

40   This is taken from Paul Le Blanc, 'Explorations in Plain Marxism,' *Revolutionary Studies: Studies in Plain Marxism* (Chicago: Haymarket Books, 2017), pp. 11, 12.

41   This point is repeated, emphasized, and elaborated by Samary, p. 163.

42   Ernest Mandel, 'The Mystifications of State Capitalism,' in *Readings on 'State Capitalism'* (London: International Marxist Group, February 1973), pp. 37-39. An elaboration of analytical perspectives shared with Mandel can be found in Janette Habel, *Cuba, The Revolution in Peril* (London: Verso, 1991). My own 2007 discussion of Cuban history and realities is offered in 'Origins and Trajectory of the Cuban Revolution,' Le Blanc, *Revolutionary Studies*, pp. 131-144. For more recent discussions, consistent with Mandel's views: Dave Kellaway, 'Fidel Dies,' *International Viewpoint* 27 November 2016 (https://internationalviewpoint. org/spip.php?article4782); Ariel Dacal Díaz, 'Notes for a Balance-Sheet of Ten Years of Reforms,' *International Viewpoint* 20 July 2018 (internationalviewpoint.org/spip.php?article5616); Fernanda Montanys, 'New Prime Minster Takes Office in Cuba,' *International Viewpoint*, 30 December 2019; (internationalviewpoint. org/spip.php?article6342); Comunistas, 'New Cuban Blog Expresses Editorial Line,' *International Viewpoint*, 20 June 2020 (internationalviewpoint.org/spip.php?article6682).

43   *Beyond Perestroika*, pp. 194-195; Ernest Mandel, *Revolutionary Marxism Today* (London: New Left Books, 1979), pp. 140, 150.

44   Samary, pp. 169-170.

45   Documentation on this can be found in David Mandel, *The Petrograd Workers in the Russian Revolution*, February

1917-June 1918 (Chicago: Haymarket Books, 2018) and Paul Le Blanc, *Lenin and the Revolutionary Party* (Chicago: Haymarket Books, 2015). It is worth noting that both works, and the challenges they suggest regarding Mandel's overly optimistic prognostication of 1989, were developed within a theoretical framework shared with and influenced by Mandel himself.

46   For example, in 'Where is America Going?' (1969) Mandel concludes that 'socialism will become a practical proposition in the United States' by the 1980s, and 'the road to revolution will then be open' (available through the Ernest Mandel Internet Archive). For balanced documents that Mandel helped craft, however, see: 'On the Current Stage of World Revolution' (1976) and 'Dictatorship of the Proletariat and Socialist Democracy' (1985) – both available on the Marxist Internet Archive.

47   *Fallacies of state capitalism* (London: Socialist Outlook, November 1991) published the debate between Ernest Mandel and Chris Harman. This is republished in this collection.

48   Trotsky, *The Workers' State and the Question of Thermidor and Bonapartism* (London, n.d.), p. 8.

49   Trotsky, *The Class Nature of the Soviet State* (London, 1962), p. 13.

50   Ibid., p. 13.

51   Ibid., p. 12.

52   Trotsky, 'Problems of the development of the USSR', *Writings, 1930-31* (New York, 1973), p. 215.

53   Trotsky, 'The Class Nature of the USSR', *Writings, 1933-4* (New York 1972), pp. 117-118.

54   Trotsky, *The Revolution Betrayed* (London, 1957), p. 286.

55   Ibid., p. 288.

56   Trotsky, *In Defence of Marxism* (New York, 1942), pp. 63-70.

57   Trotsky, *The workers' State and the Question of Thermidor and Bonapartism* (London, n.d.), p. 19.

58   Trotsky, *In Defence of Marxism*, op. cit., p. 14.

59   Trotsky, 'The War and the Fourth International', *Writings, 1939-40* (New York 1973).

60   Pablo's articles from these years are to be found in *International Secretariat Documents*, Vol. 1 (New York, 1974).

61   Letter from Deutscher to Brandler, 15 July 1953, in 'Correspondence between Brandler and Deutscher', *New Left Review*, No. 105, September-October 1977.

62   I. Deutscher, *The Prophet Unarmed* (Oxford, 1959), p. 462. See also *Universities and Left Review*, Vol. 1, No. 1, p. 10.

63   *Quatrième Internationale*, Année 14 (1956) no. 1-3.

64   E. Germain (i.e., E. Mandel), *Quatrième Internationale*, December
      1956.

65   Mandel, *Beyond Perestroika* (Verso: London 1989), p. xii.

66   Ibid., p. 116.

67   Ibid., p. 187.

68   Ibid., p. 134.

69   For instance: when he twice locates the 'Kosygin reforms' as
      beginning in the mid 1970s, whereas in fact they started ten
      years before that (see, for instance, Michael Ellman, *Socialist
      Planning* (Cambridge, 1989), pp. 73, 80, and Marshall
      Goldman, *Gorbachev's Challenge* (New York,1987), pp. 53–54);
      when he refers to Grigoriants as a 'left oppositionist', whereas he is
      a right wing liberal; when he says that 'the Congress of the Writers
      Union threw out the conservative apparatchiks in 1987', whereas
      in fact the Writers Union remained for a long time the most
      conservative of all the cultural unions.

70   Mandel, 1989, op. cit., p. xii

71   Ibid., p. 33.

72   Ibid., p. 33.

73   Ibid., p. 31.

74   Ibid., p. 34.

75   Ibid., p. 109.

76   Ibid., p. 3.

77   Ibid., p. 3.

78   Ibid., p. 32.

79   Ibid., p. 35.

80   Ibid., p. 8.

81   Ibid., p. 21.

82   For an account of this based on research in previously inaccessible
      archives, see M. Reiman, *The Birth of Stalinism* (London, 1987).

83   Vasily Selyunin, *Sotsialistischeksaya industria*, 5 January 1988.

84   Ibid.

85   Mandel, op. cit., p. 11.

86   Ibid., p. 15.

87   Ibid., p. 44.

88   Trotsky, 1962, op. cit., p. 13.

89   Mandel, op. cit., p. 62.

90   Ibid., p. 42.

91   Cliff, op. cit., p. 154.

92   Ibid.

93   Mandel, *The Inconsistencies of 'State Capitalism* (London,
     1969), p. 13.

94   *The Communist Manifesto.*

95   Bordiga, who advanced a different variant from Cliff's about
     'state capitalism' in the USSR, predicted that a general crisis
     of overproduction was going to occur in that country. He
     even announced the precise year in which it would break out.
     The year came and has long since gone. The general crisis of
     overproduction in the USSR is still awaited ...

96   The SWP comrades did not at all predict the overproduction crises
     of 1974–75 and 1980–82. We did so almost to the year in which
     they broke out.

97   It is another matter to know what period of time is needed for the
     process to have some chance of completion.

98   See the perfectly clear statement by Trotsky in *The Soviet
     Economy in Danger* (New York: Pioneer, 1933).

99   It would be better to add, the triple or quadruple pricing system,
     for account must be taken of black-market prices and of the
     'prices' (comparative advantages) of the 'grey market' (exchange
     of services).

100 In addition, the growing importance of the mass liberation
     movements in the colonial and semi-colonial countries from 1925–
     28 onwards should be included.

101 Written in 1960, *Marxist Economic Theory* (London: Merlin Press,
     1960), p. 598: 'At the same time the rates of industrial expansion
     had to be reduced', ibid. (second edition, 1969).

102 Aganbegyan claims that there was one year of absolute decline
     in production under Brezhnev. This is contradicted by every
     other source.

103 Complete and permanent monopolies are impossible under
     capitalism. The very divergence between their rates of profit and
     those in other branches inevitably attracts capital towards the
     sector that has been monopolised.

104 The Lambertists believe this. (The current led by Pierre Boussel,
     aka Pierre Lambert, was expelled from the French section of the
     Fourth International in 1953).

105 We devoted one entire chapter in *Late Capitalism* (London: Verso,
     1975) to developing this idea.

106 This is the 'rational kernel' of Keynesian and neo-Keynesian
     theories, which in every other respect are wrong.

107 See V.I. Lenin, *Imperialism, the Highest Stage of Capitalism*; N.

Bukharin, *Imperialism and the World Economy* (London, 1972); N. Bukharin, *The Economics of the Transformation Period* (New York, 1971); V.I. Lenin, 'Marginal notes to Bukharin's economics of the transformation period' in ibid.

108   Engels, *Critique of the Erfurt Programme* (Cyclostyled translation, London nd).

109   Bukharin, *Imperialism*, pp. 119–125.

110   Trotsky, *The First Five Years of the Communist International*, vol. 1 (New York, 1945), p. 23.

111   A. Amsden, 'Third World Industrialisation: 'Global Fordism' or a new model?', *New Left Review*, no.182, London, July/August 1990, p. 21.

112   Goldman and Korba, *Economic Growth in Czechoslovakia* (Prague, 1969), p. 41.

113   R. Hutchinson, 'Periodic fluctuations in Soviet historical growth rates', *Soviet Studies*, January 1969.

114   Translated in *Eastern European Economics*, vol. X, nos. 3–4.

115   B. Horvat, 'Business cycles in Yugoslavia', translated in *Eastern European Economics*, vol. IX, no. 3–4.

116   If Mandel had actually read the material produced by our organization at the time he would know that, far from supporting the idea that something called 'organized capitalism' which dispensed with these contradictions, much of our effort went into arguing with the proponents of that idea. See, for example, M. Kidron's 1956 critiques of R. Crosland and J. Strachey reprinted in *A Socialist Review*, (London, 1965) and his 'Rejoinder to left reformism' in *International Socialism* (first series), Winter 1961–2.

117   See, for example, B. Kostinsky and M. Belkindas, 'Official Soviet Gross National Product Accounting', in CIA Directorate of Intelligence, *Measuring Soviet GNP, Problems and Solutions*, (Washington 1990).

118   A. Nove, *An Economic History of the USSR* (London, 1969), p. 361.

119   See, for example, 'The future of the Russian Empire, reform or revolution', *Socialist Review* (December 1956), reprinted in *Neither Washington nor Moscow*, (London 1992), *Russia from Stalin to Kruschev*, (London, 1958); part two of the 1964 edition of *State Capitalism in Russia*, published as *Russia: a Marxist analysis*.

120   Speech translated in BBC monitoring service, 12 October 1990.

121   In P. Baran and P. Sweezy, *Monopoly Capital* (London: Harmondsworth, 1973).

122   M. Kidron and E. Dallas, 'Waste US: 1970', in M. Kidron, *Capital and Theory* (London: Pluto, 1974).

123 Figures given in W.G. Harm, *The Politics of Soviet Agriculture, 1960–1970* (Baltimore 1972), pp. 197–9 and pp. 224–25.

124 Finansy SSR 28/69.

125 For a complaint about these questions in the early Brezhnev years, see Ladenkov, *Voprosy Ekonomiki*, 1967, no. 20, translated in *Soviet Review*, vol. IX, no. 3.

126 Estimates for growth rates given in CIA Directorate of Intelligence, op. cit., pp. 110–13.

127 For one account of this example, see D.W. Conklin, 'Barriers to technological change in the USSR: the case of chemical fertilisers', *Soviet Studies*, 1969, p. 359.

128 Food and Agricultural Organization, World Agricultural Statistics, 1996, pp. 178, 176 and 11.

129 For an earlier discussion on the shortcomings of Soviet fertilisers, see D.W. Conklin, op. cit., p. 353.

130 FAO, op. cit.

131 *Pravda*, 31 October 1989.

132 *Moscow News*, 3 September 1989.

133 I. Advion suggests a 'probable' unemployment total of 8.4 million, or 6.2 per cent of the employed workforce in 'A note on the current level, pattern and trends of unemployment in the USSR', *Soviet Studies*, July 1989, p. 460.

134 The US unemployment rate in August 1990 was 5.6 per cent. International comparisons of unemployment rates are difficult to make. Nevertheless it is clear that the USSR is not qualitatively different in this respect to the West.

135 Minayeva, deputy head of All Union Central Council of Trade Unions, reported on 12 January 1989 in *Trud*.

136 See my articles, 'Poland and the Crisis of State Capitalism', in *International Socialism*, first series, nos. 93 and 94, (1976). There is a summary of my argument in the concluding chapter of my *Class Struggles in Eastern Europe* (London: Bookmarks, 1983).

137 Cliff, 'The nature of state capitalism', *Socialist Review*, March 1957, reprinted in *A Socialist Review* (London 1965).

138 The state did continue to play a role. The recessions of 1974–76 and 1980–82 were not nearly as deep as that of the 1930s. Unemployment in the early 1930s rose to one third of the workforce in the two countries where the recessions hit worst, the US and Germany. By contrast, it only rose to about 14 per cent in the worst hit Western country of the early 1980s, Britain. It is stupid of Mandel to try to ignore this by naively comparing the last two recessions not with that of interwar years, but with the average over the past 150 years – an average that reflects the vitality of capitalism's youth, not

the decay of its old age.

139 See Harman, 'The Myth of the Market', *International Socialism* 2 : 42, and 'The Storm Breaks', *International Socialism* 2 : 46.

140 E. Germain (pseudonym of Ernest Mandel) *Quatrième Internationale*, December 1956, p. 21–22.

141 Ibid., p. 23.

142 For the efforts of the CDU Interior Minister in East Germany to keep sections of Stasi functioning, see the reports in *Klassenkampf*, June 1990, p. 4, and October 1990, p. 4.

143 For a full report of these events see *Klassenkampf*, May 1990, pp. 9–11.

144 See J. Slovo, *Has Socialism Failed?* (London, 1990).

145 V. Moghadam, 'Socialism or anti-imperialism? The left and revolution in Iran', *New Left Review* no. 166, November–December 1987, p. 20.

146 'The Iranian revolution and its implications, an interview with Fred Halliday', ibid., p. 37.

147 F. Halliday, 'The ends of the Cold War', *New Left Review* no. 180, March–April 1990, pp. 12–13.

148 *New Left Review*, no. 180, p. 22.

149 *New Left Review*, no. 180, p. 18.

150 *New Left Review*, no. 180, p. 23.

151 Interview in *Marxism Today*, October 1990.

152 When its Australian section left it.

153 See Lenin's comments on Bukharin's draft party programme in Lenin: *Oeuvres*, vol. 29.

154 *Grundrisse*, p. 234 of the German edition of 1939 – our own translation.

155 Alex Callinicos, *Trotskyism* (Buckingham: Open University Press, 1990), p. 41.

156 Marx, *Theories of Surplus Value*, vol. 2, p. 510. Our stress. See likewise ibid. p. 534: 'In world market crises, all the contradictions of bourgeois production erupt collectively'

157 Callinicos, op. cit. p. 44.

158 It would be interesting to analyse the large similarity between the 'state capitalist' interpretation of contemporary capitalism and the Stalinist 'state monopolist capitalism' theory. Even more striking are parallel political conclusions concerning the absence of revolutionary perspectives in the imperialist countries for a long historical period.

159 Trotsky, 'The Soviet Economy in Danger', pp. 273-279 in *Writings of Leon Trotsky 1932* (Pathfinder Press edition).

160 The basic economic fallacy of 'socialism in one country' (later in
     one 'camp') was the illusion that the USSR could 'catch up with and
     overtake' total output, per capita output, and average productivity
     of labour of the USA and the leading capitalist industrial nations,
     i.e., maintain a higher rate of growth for an indefinite period.

161 From a certain point on, late seventies or early eighties: estimates
     differ in that respect, the US economy grew more rapidly than that
     of the USSR.

162 Of course, relative parasitism, not absolute parasitism. We take up
     that question further in this article.

163 Trotsky, *The Revolution Betrayed* (London: New Park,
     1967) pp. 275-6.

164 The top of the nomenklatura tried to prevent or at least to limit this
     indifference with regard to real costs by imposing on the managers
     different planning objectives: physical quantities of output:
     physical quantities of raw material inputs; wage costs: even net
     financial results — khozraschyot — from the mid-thirties on. But
     various objectives were contradictory and even mutually exclusive.
     In practice, the priority was given to attaining output goals in
     physical terms. And the pressure from the top went essentially in
     the same direction, as the system of bureaucratic planning had as
     its key feature the concentration of efforts on prioritised sectors
     (goals), at the expense of a proportionate development of the
     economy and society as a whole

165 Under capitalism, this is expressed most clearly in the elimination
     from cost calculations at firm level of all 'externalities' for which
     the firm does not have to pay. But even when these get a 'price',
     the socially irrational character of economic decisions measured
     in purely money terms is not suppressed. Its real character is only
     expressed more clearly. Investment decisions implying human
     deaths are considered worthwhile as long as the 'rewards' are higher
     than the costs, the 'cost' of human lives being discounted in the
     form of lost incomes. And what about the 'cost' of dead babies,
     whose potential profession and income are unknown? The inhuman
     character of this macro-social irrationality is undeniable.

166 Derek Howl, 'The law of value and the USSR', *International
     Socialism* no. 49, Winter 1990.

167 Readings on 'State Capitalism', IMG pamphlet, 1970, 1973.

168 Russia was a special case combining the character of the (most
     backward) imperialist country with that of the (most developed)
     underdeveloped country.

169 This does not represent in any way an option in favour of autarchy,
     which Trotsky systematically opposed. It represents an option in
     favour of a monopoly of foreign trade. Whether that monopoly

should be in the hands of the state or of a central organ of workers self-management bodies is another question.

170 The Theses 'Decline and Fall of Stalinism' as well as the Manifesto adopted by the 5th World Congress of the Fourth International in 1957 are entirely centred around the concept of the political revolution from below, by mass action, in the bureaucratized workers states. An editorial note appearing in the June-July 1957 issue of *Quatrième Internationale* and entitled 'From the 8th to the 9th Plenum of the Polish Workers Party' states: 'In our preceding issues, we indicated the character of the Gomulka leadership: in October (1956), it used the workers, the intellectuals and the students which rose in revolt against the police regime. But the Gomulka leadership was and remains a bureaucratic leadership, which does not try to stimulate revolution by the masses, but to channel these precisely in order to avoid revolutionary upheavals.'

171 Derek Howl, op. cit., p. 109; Harman, in *International Socialism* no. 49, pp. 80-81.

172 Leon Trotsky, *The Revolution Betrayed*, op. cit., p. 253.

173 Alex Callinicos, op. cit., p. 43.

174 V.I. Lenin, *Oeuvres*, vol. 2, p. 237. A Belgian revolutionary socialist would of course have to combine such support to a national insurrection in Belgium with unconditional support to all movements for democratic demands, including national independence, directed against Belgian imperialism in the Belgian Congo.

175 V.I. Lenin, op. cit., p. 383.

176 Alex Callinicos, op. cit., pp. 41-42.

177 Leon Trotsky, *In Defence of Marxism*, p. 99 of the original Pioneer Publishers edition.

178 Leon Trotsky, *Writings 1939-4*, Pathfinder Press original edition, pp. 217-218.

179 Contrary to the USSR under Stalin, Cuba has the most progressive working-class labour legislation of the world, more radical even than that of the Scandinavian countries or Austria.

180 It is simply not true that our French section had to wait for actions by the tiny 'state capitalist' sect in France before taking anti-fascist anti-Le Pen initiatives.

181 Karl Marx in *Marx-Engels Werke*, Band 18, p. 161.

182 It is obvious that socialists have to oppose Kinnock's witch hunt without reservations, in spite of any tactical difference they may have with this or that victim of the witch hunt. The criticism of the Militant's tactics in the Liverpool by-election is precisely that it helps Kinnock to get away with his witch hunt.

183   The SWP's tendency towards sectarianism also expresses itself
      in activity in Britain. It counterposes itself systematically to the
      Labour Party, in spite of the fact that that organization still enjoys
      the loyalty of the overwhelmingly majority of the organized
      British working class – a loyalty which could only be upset by
      a political mass radicalization which has not yet occurred. This
      leads the SWP to make recruitment to its own organization the
      main objectives of its intervention in mass struggles like the anti-
      poll tax movement.

184   'The Soviet Economy in Danger', *Writings of Leon Trotsky 1932*
      (New York: Pathfinder Press, 1973), pp. 273-274.

185   Trotsky, *The Revolution Betrayed* (New York: Pioneer Publishers,
      1937), pp. 275-276.

186   Op. cit., p. 275.

187   Op. cit., p. 289.

188   Rudolf Bahro proposes, not without justification, to replace that
      old formula with one which distinguishes between 'specific'
      and 'general' labour (i.e., mechanical labour and labour which
      is really helping to develop the human personality). He has a
      point. Especially after the technological revolution, many forms of
      intellectual labour (not to speak of administrative labour) can be
      as boring, mechanical and soul-destroying as manual conveyor-
      belt labour (indeed, there is literally an 'interoffice conveyor-belt'
      functioning already!), while certain forms of manual labour are
      obviously creative. The question is not so much that certain forms
      of mechanical labour will stay with us for a long time, even under
      socialism. It is that nobody should be restricted to performing
      such jobs, even in the period of transition between capitalism and
      socialism. Hence the key importance of a radical reduction of the
      workweek (indeed, the introduction of the half-work-week, by the
      socialist revolution). Bahro, *Eine Dokumentation* (EVA, 1977).

189   Of course, some means of production remain commodities
      in the USSR. Those sold to nonstate enterprises (kolkhozes,
      handicraft shops, foreign buyers) are the most important
      category. Small tools are also sold to individuals, and can be
      used for small scale production.

190   Those who continue to repeat that the mode of distribution has
      to 'strictly conform' to the mode of production in each and every
      social formation, according to historical materialism, we can only
      recall for the nth time Engels' statement: 'Each new mode of
      production or form of exchange is at first retarded not only by
      the old forms and the political institutions which correspond to
      them, but also by the old mode of distribution; it can secure the
      distribution which is suitable to it only in the course of a long

struggle.' Frederick Engels, *Anti-Dühring* (Moscow: Progress Publishers, 1975), p. 179.

191   This is of course not meant in the vulgar sense of accumulation of more and more material goods, but in the broader sense of creating increasing opportunities (to start with: time and material means) for individual self-development and the development of rich social relations.

192   There is no example in history of a ruling class whose basic interest would conflict with the logic of the mode of production it represents.

193   Recently, Polish managers openly stated that 'limited unemployment' wouldn't be such a bad thing to introduce more 'work discipline' into the factories.'

About the publishers

RESISTANCE BOOKS is a radical publisher of internationalist, ecosocialist, and feminist books. Resistance Books publishes books in collaboration with the International Institute for Research and Education (iire.org), and the Fourth International (https://fourth.international). For further information, including a full list of titles available and how to order them, go to the Resistance Books website.

Email: info@resistancebooks.org
Website: resistancebooks.org

THE INTERNATIONAL INSTITUTE FOR RESEARCH AND EDUCATION is a centre for the development of critical thought and the exchange of experiences and ideas between people engaged in their struggles. Since 1982, when the Institute opened in Amsterdam, it has organized courses for progressive forces around the world which deal with all subjects related to the emancipation of the oppressed and exploited. The IIRE provides activists and academics opportunities for research and education in three locations: Amsterdam, Islamabad and Manila. The IIRE publishes *Notebooks for Study and Research* in several languages. They focus on contemporary political debates, as well as themes of historical and theoretical importance.

Email: iire@iire.org
Website: iire.org

www.ingramcontent.com/pod-product-compliance
Lightning Source LLC
Chambersburg PA
CBHW032021050726
47590CB00006B/2250